Lessons in Leadership From the Bible

Lessons in Leadership From the Bible

Kenneth O. Gangel

BMH Books
Winona Lake,
Indiana 46590

The contents of this book originally appeared as a series of articles in *The Sunday School Times* and *Gospel Herald* and are adapted with permission of Union Gospel Press, Cleveland, Ohio.

Scriptural quotations in this book are from the King James and New International Versions of the Bible, the Living Bible, the New American Standard Bible, and from the author's own literal translations.

Cover design by Timothy Kennedy

ISBN: 0-88469-109-8

BMH BOOKS
WINONA LAKE, INDIANA

Printed in U.S.A.

Table of Contents

Introduction

The Bible is not a text on management just as it is not a text on science, education, or any other professional procedure. It describes people as they were—sometimes pointing out their strong points, as in the case of Solomon, and sometimes their weaknesses, as in the case of Gideon. At times Bible "heroes" display both strong and weak points (David) so we can see in crass reality the kind of relationship they sustain to God and to others. The obvious intent of the Heavenly Father is for us to extrapolate lessons from the experiences of His people through the ages.

This book is intended to do just that. The study is partially inductive—in that the author examined the lives and experiences of Bible characters to see what can be learned. But it is also deductive—in that he approached the analysis with an understanding of managerial practices, and therefore was attempting to identify those aspects of biblical leadership which can be identified with accepted contemporary procedures in management science. Hopefully the latter have not been read into the former, or superimposed upon what is really in the text.

This volume is not presented as a theology of management—that would be pretentious. It is presented as a devotional exercise for Christian leaders and administrators, enabling them to find the seeds of good managerial procedure in the Holy Scripture, which was in existence long before the founding of Harvard Business School or the American Management Association.

Serious study of Christian leadership does not begin with textbooks, but with the text of the Bible; and though a great deal can be learned from the didactic portions, a biographical approach to leadership study is most profitable. Let us see, then, what God has done to create and use leaders through all the ages of the past, and learn how He can reproduce those qualities in us today.

KOG
Miami, Florida

Joseph: Long-Range Planning

In the twentieth century there has been a proliferation of literature dealing with the science of leadership and administration. Yet many of the lessons demonstrated in modern texts on leadership can be found in seed form in the pages of the Bible. Of course, Scripture is no more a textbook on leadership than it is on science. But the very examples of men and women whom God gifted and used in leadership positions offer us a wealth of information as to how we can exercise leadership in our day.

Our first lesson comes from the life of Joseph, who is one of the outstanding leaders in the Book of Genesis. It is a lesson on long-range planning. Young Joseph went to Egypt shortly after 1900 B.C. Through a series of events which surely must have seemed unfortunate to Joseph at the time, he found himself languishing in prison after a very promising start as the chief steward in Potiphar's household.

Joseph spent a long time in that prison, seemingly accomplishing nothing. Even after the chief butler had been restored to his position in the palace, Joseph waited two more years. It is precisely Joseph's experience in prison that leads us to our first lesson from his life and leadership.

Long-Range Planning Requires a Qualified Planner

Who would have thought that God, in His infinite wisdom, would design college training for Joseph in the depths of prison? Other Bible leaders had similar experiences–such as Moses on the back side of the desert, Paul in the wilderness, and Joshua in his years as a leader under Moses.

One of the requirements for a qualified planner is experience, and Joseph was gaining some very valuable experience in a most unlikely place. First of all, he held a position of responsibility in prison (Gen. 39:22-23). Second, the qualities of patience, serenity of spirit, and maturity of judgment were being built into the young man's life during those long days and nights.

A second qualification which Joseph illustrated as a planner is wisdom. It very well may be that some of this wisdom was pounded into Joseph during his years in prison, but more likely it represented a gift from God.

Joseph demonstrated his wisdom by interpreting Pharaoh's dream as a message from God regarding seven years of prosperity followed by seven years of famine. Then he said to the monarch, "My suggestion is that you find the wisest man in Egypt and put him in charge of administering a nationwide farm program" (Gen. 41:33 Living Bible). Pharaoh's response at the end of Joseph's consultation indicates that, in his judgment, Joseph was already the wisest man in Egypt. Therefore, Pharaoh need look no farther for the kind of wisdom necessary to implement this massive plan.

Still a third qualification of a planner as illustrated by Joseph is the spiritual gift of administration. The Greek word *kuberneseis* appears in 1 Corinthians 12:28 and there identifies a specific gift for ministry which relates to administration. The word itself comes from the idea of directing the activities of a ship, or even a shipping company. But Paul used it in the context of spiritual gifts–to specify that kind of ministry which has to do with directing the affairs of a church, of which one of the most important aspects is long-range planning.

So Pharaoh should get some points for wisdom himself for saying, " 'Who could do it better than Joseph? For he is a man who is obviously filled with the Spirit of God' " (Gen. 41:38 Living Bible).

The necessity of a qualified planner to carry out long-range planning is no less important today than it was in ancient Egypt. Whether we are talking about a five-year plan for the Sunday school or a ten-year plan for a college, we need to find men and women whom God has prepared to carry out this kind of planning. They must have and be able to exercise the virtues of experience and wisdom and the gift of administration.

Long-Range Planning Requires Futuristic Commitment

It is interesting that Joseph's handling of Pharaoh's dream was based, at least in part, upon his philosophy of history. Joseph expressed confidence that God was in charge of history and the land of Egypt (see Gen. 41:25, 32). God had decided to show Pharaoh what He was going to do, and Pharaoh could be sure that He would do it and that He would do it shortly.

I am reminded of a definition of the sovereignty of God, which is frequently used by a pastor friend of mine: "The sovereignty of God simply means that God knows what He's doing and He's doing it."

The planner with a biblical futuristic commitment does not see his present responsibilities abrogated by his understanding of prophecy regarding the return of the Lord. Rather, he sees a constant responsibility to be working while watching. The business of selling all one's property, clothing oneself in a white sheet, and climbing to the top of a nearby mountain to wait for the return of the Lord is a practice of cultic sectarianism. It is not worthy of those who take the Scriptures seriously.

Long-Range Planning Requires Accurate Information

The only intelligent way to prognosticate about the future is to find out as much as possible about the past and the present. That is why it is much more difficult to do long-range planning for a new church or organization than for one which has some background or history.

In order to obtain the data which he needs, the planner must have the authority to get it; and that is exactly what Joseph had: "And Pharaoh said unto Joseph, Forasmuch as God hath shewed thee all this, there is none so discreet and wise as thou art: Thou shalt be over my house, and according unto thy word shall all my people be ruled: only in the throne will I be greater than thou. And Pharaoh said unto Joseph, See, I have set thee over all the land of Egypt" (Gen. 41:39-41).

If your supervisor or board is expecting you to take responsibility for long-range planning, make sure it is understood that it will be essential for you to have access to whatever information is necessary in order to project the kind of plan which will carry the institution through the days and years of the future.

A second factor with respect to accurate information is the necessity of working to find it. The Scripture says that after Joseph's appointment, he "went out from the presence of Pharaoh, and began traveling all across the land" (Gen. 41:46 Living Bible).

Sometimes the information is not immediately accessible to the planner. In Joseph's case, a great deal of traveling and footwork were required for him to see for himself exactly what condition Egypt was in. In our day it is more likely that the planner will get information from subordinates, from existing records, or perhaps even from a computer printout. But the principle is the same—long-range planning does not operate in a vacuum of information.

After he has reasonably accurate information about the organization's past and present, the administrative planner has to have the sense to utilize it. In Genesis 47:13-26, we read the details of how, when the famine became severe all across the Mediterranean world, Joseph first gathered up all the money, then all the land, and eventually the people themselves for Pharaoh.

From the democratic point of view, this looks like a repressive autocracy on the part of Joseph; and we wonder how he could have been led to such austere ends by God's Holy Spirit. But let us not superimpose our cultural standard on the historical setting of the passage. This was Egypt, not North America, and it was 1900 B.C., not A.D. 1980. It all made perfectly good sense, considering the cultural standards of the day; and it was, no doubt, precisely what God instructed Joseph to do.

Long-Range Planning Requires Practical Implementation

There must always be, in every plan, what I like to call *realization procedures.* Sometimes objectives tend to be very fuzzy, and therefore plans are ambiguous.

In Genesis 41:33-35, Joseph mapped out the kind of organization necessary to make the plan work: there must be one man at the top making the basic decisions; there must be overseers directing the storing of one-fifth of the harvest for the first seven years; the food must be gathered into certain strategically located storage cities; and there must be provision for a plan of distribution as it is needed. So the first ingredient of practical implementation is *specificity of the plan.*

A second factor of importance is *delegation.* Pharaoh delegated to Joseph, who in turn delegated to certain selected leaders. The lines of authority were maintained throughout the administrative organization. In Genesis 41:55, we learn how much keen administrative insight Pharaoh himself had because when people asked him questions about the program, he simply told them to go to Joseph and do whatever he told them.

The Scripture also tells us that Joseph had control over the procedures (see Gen. 41:56-57). Still another area relating to practical implementation was Joseph's built-in *corrective measures* for problem solving. These appear primarily in Genesis 47:1-31, where we see more and more people coming for more and more help. Joseph apparently had designed sufficient flexibility into the long-range plan that he could meet each contingency as it came along.

The results of Joseph's efforts were at least threefold: the nation of Egypt was saved, the fledgling family-nation of Israel was saved, and Joseph himself was saved. Actually the order is just a bit different from that, because God saved Joseph in order to save Egypt in order to save Israel, the nation from which His Messiah was to come.

So let us no longer think of Joseph only as a frightened boy thrown into a pit by his brothers or as a strange psychic who could interpret dreams. He was one of the most astute administrative leaders in all of history, and the Scriptures offer in some detail the account of his efforts in long-range planning.

Moses: Politics or Power

The decade of the 70s has been an agonizing one in the political fabric of the world. During this decade, several major Western nations–Canada, France, Germany, and the United States–have been either without leadership or have had heads of state in extreme difficulty. Perhaps never before in this century has a leadership vacuum been so acute and so obvious.

It is encouraging for Christians, in such an era of international chaos, to turn again to Scripture for a fresh glimpse of how God makes leaders. The dynamic career of Moses, by most measurements the greatest leader of the Old Testament, affords us a remarkable demonstration of how God's value system is strikingly different from ours.

The name of Moses' father was Amram; and of his mother, Jochebed (see Exod. 6:20). They were a simple, but devout, couple whose only defense against Pharaoh's butchery was to float their baby in a basket on the river in the hope that God would somehow hear their prayer for his deliverance. So the very existence of Moses was contrived in faith (see Heb. 11:23).

For the next 40 years, life must have been difficult and dichotomous for young Moses. On the one hand, his own mother taught him the faith of Jehovah and sensitivity to the spiritual and physical plight of his people. On the other hand, Scripture records that he was "learned in all the wisdom of the Egyptians, and was mighty in words and in deeds" (Acts 7:22). The effect of Jochebed's humble teaching upon Moses as he spent his years in the pagan universities of Egypt ought to be a positive model for Christian parents today.

James Montgomery Boice says of the education Moses received in Egypt:

> By means of hieroglyphic and more popular cuneiform systems of writing, Egyptian learning thrived in the second millennium B.C. Heliopolis was a center of scribal and priestly learning. Presumably Moses was instructed in reading and writing, thereby developing the skills that he wished to use later in drafting the first five books of the Bible.[1]

There was a day, of course, when Moses had to decide between the politics of Egypt and the power of God. In our day it is possible to be a Christian politician, although the role must surely be a difficult one. And in a time before Moses, Joseph somehow mixed purity with politics in the very same country.

But this was a different era, and there was no way to harmonize the political future open to him as an adopted prince with the plight of the slave people from whom he had come. Scripture records:

> By faith Moses, when he had grown up, refused to be known as the son of Pharaoh's daughter. He chose to be mistreated along with the people of God rather than to enjoy the pleasures of sin for a short time. He regarded disgrace for the sake of Christ as of greater value than the treasures of Egypt, because he was looking ahead to his reward (Heb. 11:24-26 NIV).

In making that decision, Moses has set for us the precedent of choosing spiritual power rather than worldly politics as a leadership style. Here are some of the results of his decision.

He Learned That Leadership Was Impossible in His Own Strength

Exodus 2:11-14 records a scene not unlike so-called early American frontier justice. No doubt Moses thought he was doing right to kill the Egyptian, but his act was neither in God's timing nor according to God's way. There is no indication in the text that the young prince sought the mind of Jehovah as to how he could be used to accomplish the ends he felt were noble. He took matters into his own hands. Then, in the name of patriotism and justice, he committed a murder. One is reminded of how Peter acted on impulse in the garden and hacked off the ear of the high priest's servant (see John 18:10).

Dewey Beegle suggests: "Moses must have had a strong ego as well, because the flush of victory pulled him back the next day. He had removed one threat to his people and perhaps he could be of assistance again."[2]

Moses' strange combination of Hebrew theology and Egyptian politics had not yet prepared him to do the work of God; now in fear and apparent defeat, he ran off into exile.

He Profited from His Failures

This is an extremely important lesson in leadership. Every leader knows that discouragements come and the decisions which he makes will, on occasion, not be the best ones. But once a bad judgment and the problems caused by it become reality, the next step is to profit from one's mistakes. God enabled Moses to do just that.

Though Moses may come under some criticism for his multiple excuses in evading God's call, one thing is clear—he had learned humility and a complete dependence on Jehovah, rather than on himself.

It is a different Moses we encounter in Exodus 3:11 as he says, "Who am I?" Now he voiced almost the same expression as had been thrown at him by one of the Hebrew slaves on that second day he sauntered out as their deliverer (see 2:14).

James Murphy suggests the reasons for Moses' attitude of unworthiness:

> He remembered the grandeur of the court and the haughtiness of the monarch. He was aware that the present sovereign was a stranger to him. He called to mind the rude reception he had met from one of his own kinsmen when he formerly interfered in their behalf. All the difficulties of the enterprise crowded on his mind, and he felt himself inadequate to his achievement.[3]

Whatever else maturity may do for us, it ought to make us aware of our own inadequacies and therefore more patient with the inadequacies of those less experienced than we are. The haughty dogmatism which so often characterizes young leaders in the church tends to pass with years of experiencing failure as well as success in one's leadership role.

He Recognized His Own Call and Commission from God

When Moses returned to Egypt, he went as an apostle—one sent with a message. The account in Exodus emphasizes repeatedly that Moses did as the Lord commanded him. There was no room for creative expression here.

This was a serious confrontation between the God of heaven and the pagan deities of Egypt. Moses and Pharaoh, Israel and Egypt—these were only the intermediaries through which the real conflict was being played out.

Moses would never have been able to endure the pressures of a confrontation with Pharaoh had he not been in constant awareness that he was doing precisely what God had called him to do. The same is true of his later adventures in the wilderness.

That same awareness is important in church leadership today. Pastors, superintendents, board members, teachers, and other church leaders must be able to stand confidently before friend and foe alike in the call and commission of the Lord. Moses was doing it *God's* way now, and there is something about that kind of confidence which can give even an 80-year-old shepherd dramatic courage in the court of the most powerful king of his day.

He Persevered against All Criticism and Adversity

Every leader knows that when things are going well, he stands to receive plaudits from his followers; but that when things are not going well, he will be the immediate target of every complaint. Some form of the word "murmur" appears at least eight times in Exodus 16:1-12. Rather than thanking Moses for delivering them from bondage, the Children of Israel constantly complained about the food, the desert, and the leadership of Moses.

But in all this, Moses somehow managed to stay in control of himself most of the time. William Sanford LaSor says:

> Only once in all the wilderness journey, only once did Moses seem to lose his patience, and that is in the story in the twentieth chapter of Numbers where he smote the rock in impatience to bring forth the water for them. He was, indeed, a man of long-suffering and faith and intercession![4]

He Showed a Tender and Warm Heart for His People

Perhaps the secret of Moses' patience and perseverance was that he really loved the Children of Israel. When their doctrinal apostasy surpassed even their daily complaining, Jehovah threatened to cut them off and start all over again with Moses in the place of Abraham. But rather than endorse such a plan, Moses reminded God of His promises to the patriarchs (see Exod. 32:13).

In Exodus 32:32, the great leader went so far as to offer himself as a substitutionary representative for the people. He was willing to give up whatever eternal status he might have with Jehovah if God would let His people live.

He Was in Constant Touch with God

Moses was a personal friend of the God of the Bible. Such a relationship is almost inconceivable—at least before the incarnation. But Exodus 34:1-9 indicates how intimate was the friendship of the man and his God. By no means do we find that intimacy mentioned only there; it is the essential theme of much of the Pentateuch. Exodus 33:11 really tells the story: "And the Lord spake unto Moses face to face, as a man speaketh unto his friend."

How important this sensitive communication is for us as leaders in the church! How basic that our people should expect us to have been with God in a very real way! A literal replay of these chapters may be too much to expect in an age of grace with the completed canon of Scripture at our fingertips. But nevertheless, through prayer and the constant monitoring of the Holy Spirit, we certainly are (or should be) those who maintain constant contact with the throne room of heaven.

We almost feel as though the story of Moses should end with him triumphantly leading the Children of Israel over Jordan into the land of Canaan. But he forfeited that right in a moment of anger, and all that remained was to look at the Promised Land. There is a lesson even in the death of Moses—a lesson about how serious God considers sin in His appointed leaders.

The choice between politics and power spanned a career of 80 years of preparation followed by 40 years of active service in the ministry of Jehovah. The lessons in faith, prayer, obedience, and meekness are worthy of careful study by any leader in the church today.

Jethro: First Management Consultant

Exodus 18 is one of the most important chapters in the entire Bible on the subject of administrative leadership. It pictures Moses and his host of exiles just recently separated from Egypt, and getting settled in the wilderness. Jethro, priest of Midian and father-in-law of Moses, made a visit to his son-in-law. The recent development was something Jethro had never anticipated during Moses' 40 years of living with the family in Midian.

We know very little about Jethro—he was apparently a wise man, and was probably a believer in Jehovah (although that cannot be established for sure). William Sanford LaSor wrote of Jethro: "It may well be that the knowledge of Jehovah was part of his heritage, and that in his household, Moses learned to realize more about what the worship of Jehovah involves."[1]

Remember that Jethro could have had a direct contact to Jehovah through the line of Midian, who was a son of Abraham by Keturah (see Gen. 25:1-2). It is clear in Exodus

18:7-26 that Moses welcomed his father-in-law, thought highly of his advice, and immediately implemented his suggestion.

In the narrative of Exodus 18 we see almost all the issues of delegation, in a general sense, which management science has uncovered and written in specifics during the past 30 or 40 years. Once again, the researchers could have saved time and money by first checking God's Word.

Delegation Does Not Come Naturally to a Leader

Exodus 18:13 is a classic picture of traditional autocratic leadership. It pictures a long line of people standing from morning until night waiting to get to talk to the only man who had authority and wisdom enough to handle their problems.

It apparently had never occurred to Moses that some of the responsibilities he was taking to himself were duties which could very well be assigned to other men. He said very bluntly: "I judge between one and another, and I do make them know the statutes of God, and his laws" (Exod. 18:16).

This attitude is all too characteristic of many leaders in our day. The "strong pastor" idea is a gentle way of referring to the monarchical form of leadership characteristic of the kings of the Gentiles in Jesus' day, but repudiated by the Lord for use in the Church (see Luke 22:24-27).

Failure to delegate is not a logical problem, but an emotional one. All the logic which a leader can apply to his own use of time, physical endurance, and the achievement of work responsibilities would lead him to opt for delegation. His failure to do so stems from an underestimation of what others can contribute to the total ministry of the organization.

Delegation Is Essential for Survival

It took wise Jethro just one glance to discover that Moses' system would never do. His words are a classic statement of the meaning of delegation: "Thou wilt surely wear away, both thou, and this people that is with thee: for this thing is too heavy for thee; thou art not able to perform it thyself alone" (Exod. 18:18).

Not only was Moses overburdened by his failure to delegate, but he was defeating leadership development among the people. One management periodical states the issue very clearly:

> Lack of people qualified for delegation and greater responsibilities can rarely be blamed on others. Your help in many ways to encourage an employee's growth will not only help you to get your work done but help with an attitude which will motivate him to want to give greater assistance. This obviously requires time–but there's great payoff to every one related to the company.[2]

So a Sunday school superintendent who has had no training in leadership or administration may want to seek some help in seminars, or at least do some serious reading on the process of delegation. Mature leadership is not an inherent ability, but a learned behavior. If one has the gift of administration, he still has the responsibility for developing that gift.

Delegation Is a Biblical and Spiritual Technique

Frequently when I talk about management processes such as delegation, someone suggests that these are human ploys which will subvert the real working of the Spirit of God. Certainly there is a possibility that one can substitute human ability or expertise for spiritual power and divine guidance. But that is not always the case–and certainly does not have to be. One reason for developing a series of lessons in leadership from the Scriptures is to show how many of the things taught in administration science today are actually biblical principles.

Jethro never intended that Moses should violate God's word in listening to the advice of his father-in-law. Exodus 18:19 might very well be translated, "I will give you advice in order that God may be with you." The Holy Spirit could speak to and through Jethro just as He could speak through Moses. Moses is a good model here for willingness on the part of an established leader to listen to what others have to tell him.

The Scripture offers no criticism of Moses for heeding Jethro's advice, and God did bless Moses when he followed that advice. God uses many means to direct His servants, and the wise counsel of interested friends is not the least of His means.

Delegation Does Not Abrogate the Leader's Responsibility

In delegating the work, Moses was not handing over the *responsibility* God had given him. He was making himself and the people more effective by organizing the responsibility correctly. It was still his task to teach and demonstrate the way the people should walk and the work they should do. He even selected the men who would hold the place of responsibility and to whom he would delegate some of the work load.

Someone has said that a leader can and should delegate responsibility and the authority to carry out that responsibility, but he cannot ultimately delegate *accountability* for the task. In other words, if a subordinate fails, it may be the delegating leader's task to discipline that subordinate or at least help him to be more competent at his task. But in answering to his own superior, that leader must bear the responsibility for what the subordinate failed to do. It is this built-in accountability that makes delegation such a risky business in the eyes of some.

Delegation Should Be Practiced Only with Qualified Personnel

There is no gain to the leader or the subordinate when the task delegated is greater than the ability of the one who bears it. Consequently, the Holy Spirit gives wisdom to leaders who trust Him to discern which tasks can be carried out by which people. Members of a Christian education committee face this kind of responsibility all the time—as do pastors, ministers of Christian education, and Sunday school superintendents. My guess would be that the men who were "rulers of thousands" demonstrated greater leadership qualities than those who were "rulers of tens" (see Exod. 18:21).

This does not mean that one should use only a small minority of people to accomplish tasks. The management periodical referred to earlier reminds us that "the manager will never get more such people if he doesn't take the risks and see that all of his people are given the opportunities to learn leadership within the tried and true category."

Please notice that we are not looking here at leadership qualifications only in a general sense. Jethro was suggesting that these men be more than just able. They had to be men who feared God, who held the truth in sincerity, and who hated covetousness (see Exod. 18:21). Elevating persons without spiritual qualifications to positions of leadership in a religious organization would be very dangerous business, and Jethro wisely warned against such a practice.

Delegation Requires a Span of Control

The phrase "span of control" has to do with the number of persons over whom a leader has responsibility, and for whose activities he can be held accountable. They are his subordinates in the technical sense, and they answer to him for their activities. J. P. Hyatt wrote of this passage:

> This may be the heart of Jethro's practical advice. Moses was to decide the more important and more difficult matters, perhaps especially those requiring consultation of the divine oracle, whereas the lesser judges were to decide the lesser cases for which there was known precedent and custom. . . . This probably does not mean simple distinction between "religious" and "civic" cases.[3]

As God is a God of order and design, so His earthly leaders ought to be people of order and design. This carefully constructed organizational package which Jethro proposed was hardly a bureaucracy in any sophisticated sense. The flow of communication is clearly provided for. Persons who really had to have access to Moses were still able to get there–and now without waiting for three or four days in the hot desert sun.

Delegation Results in a Harmonious Organization

Jethro was willing to put his consultation on the evaluation scale of results. If God commended the advice and Moses implemented it, then there would be harmony and peace in the camp (see Exod. 18:23). Moses apparently felt that this was the will of God and put the plan into operation immediately.

Delegation can help you a great deal in your leadership responsibilities. Study Exodus 18, read supplementary literature on the subject, trust the Spirit of God to give you understanding of delegation, and implement it in a flexible way, being willing to adapt and change as the need demands.

Joshua: Paying the Price of Preparation

4

As the Book of Joshua opens, we sense immediately that it was the end of an era—Moses had died. The 40 years of wilderness wandering had come to a close, and we notice only two men still remaining who had been with Moses from the earliest days of the exodus. For 40 years, Caleb and Joshua had served and learned in the shadow of the great leader. Now God was about to elect one of them to take Moses' place.

Joshua first entered the biblical record as a general in the battle against Amalek under Moses, his commander in chief. Aaron and Hur stood on a hill holding up Moses' hands in obedience to the Lord's conditional promise (see Exod. 17:8-13). Later we find that Joshua joined the inner circle of command and accompanied Moses up Mount Sinai instead of Aaron and Hur (see Exod. 24:13).

He appears in Numbers 13:8, 16 as one of the spies sent into Canaan; and later it is recorded that he was put in charge of the division of land among the tribes (see Num. 34:17).

His rise up the ladder of leadership was steady and apparently related to his complete faithfulness at every point.

Although the Book of Joshua contains many lessons in leadership, our particular focus is on the book's first nine verses—which clearly identify the way Jehovah placed this man into a position of important leadership. The characteristics which we see in Joshua are certainly appropriate to church leaders in our day.

Preparation Presupposes a Distinct Call

God's call of Joshua to service is recorded in Joshua 1:1. The new leader did not attempt to wrest leadership from Moses at any time during their 40 years together. There is no evidence that he ever envied or lusted after the top position. He served under Moses throughout the years with little apparent concern for his own career.

Josephus, the Jewish historian, suggested that Joshua had already lived 40 years in Egyptian slavery before he joined the exodus. If that is correct, then Joshua's preparational period had gone on for no less than 80 years—precisely the same amount of time God used to bring Moses to the point of ultimate leadership.

Surely it would have seemed natural for the Children of Israel to thrust Joshua into leadership when Moses was gone. He was the logical man. But God does not always work according to human logic, as Samuel discovered in selecting a replacement for Saul from among Jesse's sons. It was divine appointment, not human popularity, which brought Joshua to responsibility.

No doubt many times during those 40 years Joshua wondered what the future held for him. There may have been times when his tasks seemed menial and unimportant, but yet he persevered as "Moses' minister" (Joshua 1:1).

The most strategic factor in Joshua's preparation was his sensitivity to the call of God. Alan Redpath wrote:

> Joshua knew perfectly well that Canaan was infested by a thousand foes. He knew that every inch of advance would be contested by the enemy. But a man assured of the call of God is invincible. Certainly he is very conscious of his deficiencies; he is aware of all of the walled cities in the land and of the broad river that he has to cross before he gets there. He knows something of the ridicule and the criticism which are forever the portion of those who would dare to stand for God. But looking away from all these to the revealed purpose of God, he gives himself utterly and completely to the channel through which the divine will may be worked out![1]

Preparation Requires Patience

We have already noted the number of years Joshua spent in secondary roles waiting for God's time. Now as we consider Joshua 1:2, let us consider that it was probably *because* of these years, rather than *in spite of* them, that Joshua was able to enter his leadership role with the quality of patience.

When the multitudes rebelled against Moses and against God in the wilderness, Joshua never joined their ranks. When the hearts of the majority of the spies failed them because of the giants in the land, Joshua, along with Caleb, stood firm in commitment to God's ability.

The Scripture records that Joshua had "wholly followed the Lord" (Num. 32:12). He was a symbol to the entire new generation that it was indeed possible to wait for God's time and to stay faithful to Him in the most difficult of circumstances.

It is very easy to pass over the words "now therefore" (Joshua 1:2) unless we remember what kind of a turning point they meant in the life of Joshua. We could almost substitute the word "finally." I think it was Abraham Lincoln who was asked about his aspirations as a young political leader and said: "I will prepare myself and be ready; perhaps my chance will come."

Preparation Demands Dependability and Dependence

As we read Joshua 1:3-5, we should remember that God did not call Joshua to handle the task alone. Just as Moses had full assurance by the burning bush that Jehovah was in complete command of any situation which might arise, so now He assured Joshua that it would be His task, not Joshua's, to give the people the land. What a wonderful promise we find at the end of verse 5: "... as I was with Moses, so I will be with thee: I will not fail thee, nor forsake thee."

Leadership demands dependability, but Christian leadership demands dependence as well. In fact, part of the dependability of leadership is a commitment to dependence on the God of the Bible.

King Saul ceased being dependable when he failed to be dependent. As soon as he felt that he could stand in the place of Samuel in making sacrifices, or second-guess God in sparing those who God commanded that he kill, his usefulness was finished.

Joshua made no excuses, as did Moses. But then, Joshua had had ample opportunity to see the God of Israel in action. He served the miracle-working Jehovah, and he knew it.

An exact comparison of the leadership of Joshua with that of Moses is almost impossible. There were differences in the situation, people, need, and man. But one thing is clear: Joshua paid the price of preparation, as Moses did, learning dependability and dependence on the Lord.

Preparation Provides Courage

Anyone who has served in a position of leadership appreciates God's reminder to His new earthly commander in Joshua 1:6-7.

Leadership requires courage. The battles of the future were to be much more severe and demanding than the battles of the past. Joshua had been a man under orders, implementing the decisions made by Moses. Now he faced the responsibility of top executive leadership, the making of crucial decisions affecting not only his own life, but the lives of many other people.

In the Scriptures, God often repeats things He wants to emphasize; so He says three times in verses 1-9 that Joshua must be strong and courageous for his leadership role.

Joshua stood on the veritable bank of the Jordan knowing as no one else could know (except Caleb) what awaited the people on the other side of the river. This was not the first time God had singled out Joshua for leadership, nor was it the first time He had reminded him that courage would be necessary (see Num. 27:18-21; Deut. 31:14-23). But it was the first time that Joshua had ever understood the mighty task for which God had been preparing him these many years.

Preparation Affords Time to Learn the Word

Every man God used in Bible times, whether in the Old or New Testaments, was a man who knew the Word of God. Such is the application of Joshua 1:8-9 for today. Sometimes that Word was directly spoken, as in the cases of Abraham and Moses. At other times, it was the written Word, as in the cases of Joshua and most of the leaders after him.

Amid the crushing responsibility of military administration, Joshua was to be a theologian, constantly meditating in the written law and aware that its teachings led to prosperity and success as measured by Jehovah.

What a marvelous lesson for today is the dynamic of Christian leadership as resident in the supernatural combination of the Spirit and the Word! Pastors, superintendents, educational leaders, and church workers at all levels must saturate themselves in God's Holy Book to be genuinely prepared for leadership. Redpath puts it this way:

> There is a price to be paid. Are you willing to pay it? Cancel every responsibility in your life other than what you believe to be God's will for you. Deliberately refuse any engagement which will

> keep you from meditation on His Word. We are living in an age which has lost the art of being silent with an open Bible and waiting for God to speak.[2]

The Price of Preparation

Paying the price of preparation is a crucial lesson of leadership. This truth is also suggested to us by applying Joshua 1:8-9 to today. Sometimes new converts are so eager to serve God that they want to rush into important positions of church leadership without adequate time to allow God an opportunity to mold them for those positions.

Sometimes a distorted viewpoint of eschatology leads us to frantically try crash programs of ministry so that we can get the task done before Jesus comes again. To be sure, His coming is imminent, but if we are walking in God's will, we will also be walking in God's timing.

Preparation must not be ignored. What a marvelous example Joshua is! William Sanford LaSor reminds us:

> Few men, if any, step into responsible positions without preparation. Sometimes in our shortsightedness we seem to get the idea in regard to Bible characters that they come on the scene ready-made, fully prepared; here they are, God's gift to the world! They take up the work, and that is all there is to it. But if you will read more carefully, you will find that usually—I think we could even say always—there is a period of preparation behind them. God lays His plans well in advance.[3]

Gideon: Learning the Role of Faith

After the work of Barak and Deborah, the Scripture tells us that the land had rest for 40 years (see Judges 5:31). Although freedom and safety had been earned from the king of Canaan (see Judges 4:24), there was still a constant terror of roving robber bands of Midianites. The ill-equipped and divided tribes of Israel were no match for the constant invaders they experienced during these years of the judges. The Bible reminds us, "There was no king in Israel: every man did that which was right in his own eyes" (Judges 21:25).

Throughout the years of its history, the nation of Israel continuously had problems with the worship of the Canaanite god, Baal.

This god figures prominently in the story of Gideon. The narrator of the story records that the Midianite hordes slashed into Israelite territory just about harvesttime and chopped down everything in their way, leaving the people to starve. Kittel describes the scene accurately:

> The Midian hordes that had not crossed the Jordan at Beth-shean and from there invaded the plain of Jezreel found a second estuary of the Jordan at Adam (now Tell-eddamie) at the confluence of the Jabbok and the Jordan. From there through the Wadi Fara, which extends northwest in the direction of Shechem, they advanced toward the interior mountain region.[1]

The Haunting Issue of Doubt

One can hardly blame Gideon for lack of faith during the difficult times in which he lived. His response to the words of the angel was a logical one: "If the Lord is with us, why then has all this happened to us? And where are all His miracles which our fathers told us about, saying, 'Did not the Lord bring us up from Egypt?' But now the Lord has abandoned us and given us into the hand of Midian" (Judges 6:13 NASB).

It seemed to Gideon that God was mocking the plight of Israel. Gideon had no difficulty believing in the reality of the angel, and openly carried on a conversation with him. But to believe that God still cared for His people, when all around him Gideon could see nothing but starvation and ruin, was too much for the young man.

But as the angel spoke, Gideon came to a different response, and pleaded for someone else to have the responsibility (Judges 6:15). His family was poor, and he was the youngest of all. Gideon's doubt lay not only in the question of God's genuine care for Israel, but also in his failure to find any evidence of leadership in himself. At this point he was not unlike Moses, who had great difficulty believing that God really wanted to use one such as he.

Finally, like a true Jew, Gideon wanted some specific sign that God was indeed speaking to him in some unique way. He asked the angel to remain until he brought some kind of offering. If the one with whom he was speaking ate the food, that would be evidence that he had not just seen a vision or had a dream of this very important conversation.

Leadership in the church today often begins much like Gideon's leadership began. We do not consider ourselves worthy of the call of God. We question the validity of our own spiritual gifts, and wonder whether leaders in the church have made a wise selection when they ask us to do something. The ultimate issue of importance is a recognition that this kind of selection has come from God.

The Strengthening Signs of Confirmation

At two points in his rise to leadership in Israel, Gideon requested some physical sign from God to confirm his call. The first of these hardly went as he expected—but it was, nevertheless, a sign. The food which he brought to the angel of the Lord was not eaten by his heavenly visitor. Instead, the angel of the Lord reached out the end of his staff, touched the meat and the unleavened cakes, and fire came up out of a bare rock to consume the entire offering. At this point, the angel of the Lord disappeared.

Between this confirming sign and the next, Gideon took his first act of leadership—by tearing down the altar of Baal and erecting an altar to the Lord. But even yet, his leadership radiated a basic timidity—perhaps even fear—because he did not tackle these tasks by day. He secretly carried out his mission at night.

It is, of course, a credit to Joash that he defended his son on the logical grounds that if Baal were really a god, he could take care of himself—it ought not to be the task of the people to care for him. The conversation between Joash and his neighbors is characteristic of how deep into Baal worship the people had sunk at this point in their history.

The second sign given Gideon was the one with which we are generally familiar—the wet and dry fleece. It is interesting how one can sermonize on this passage—by emphasizing Gideon's wisdom in requesting a sign, or his ungrateful, faithless sin in doing so.

I think it is noteworthy that the Scripture never condemns Gideon for this act, though, no doubt, God would have eventually given him the courage, even without this physical sign.

I am frequently impressed with the fact that God seems to be more flexible with people than we are. We are quick to condemn Bible characters for behavior that is never censured in Scripture. (Consider the vow of Jephthah in Judges 11.)

At any rate, Gideon achieved his goal of confidence in God's call and in God's willingness to support the battle. Let's remember that Gideon was accustomed to poverty and fear as a life style. No doubt when it came to an analysis of leadership characteristics, he could hardly find in himself the qualifications to lead a group of farmers, all probably less equipped then he, to battle against the Midianite hordes.

Hastings says of Gideon:

> He was a thoughtful man who had difficulties other men had not. But now, having again been granted a sign, his mind was made up. He believed he had been called of God to fight his country's battles. We never again read of a sign asked. He knows whom he is trusting.[2]

The Clear Pattern of God's Provision

We know Gideon best for the battle with the pitchers and lamps, and notably for the *preparation* for that battle. No one who was afraid was allowed to accompany Gideon–because this was a battle of faith and courage. But even when 22,000 admitted to fear (and again, God does not condemn them for that honest emotion), there were still 10,000 left. But God wanted to show His people that He alone would win the battle. So, with a unique method–the "lappers" and the "non-lappers"–God selected those whom He wanted to fight. Finally, 300 remained; and the battle was set in array. God gave Gideon one more experience of encouragement–Gideon heard the story of the dream told around the campfire in the Midianite camp.

Perhaps the dynamic lesson of leadership in this portion of Judges 6-8 is God's complete ability to care for our needs in leadership positions. We tend to measure strength in human terms–how much money we have in the budget, how many people we can put into the task, and what physical resources are available. All these are important; and they are things which leaders ought to be thinking about. But above and beyond these is the power of God to conquer the Midianite camp with 300 ill-trained, but faithful warriors. It is interesting how God uses human logic and natural events, on occasion, to accomplish His purposes. What better way was there for 300 men without weapons to win a battle than by convincing the enemy that they were greatly outnumbered? God, in His wisdom, created the confusion that ultimately led to the self-destruction of the Midianites.

Like so many times in Israel's history, both before and after the days of Gideon, the battle was the Lord's. It is to Gideon's credit, despite the degeneration of his leadership after the Midianite victory, that he reminded the people that the Lord was their real leader, and the one who would rule over them (see Judges 8:23).

The Dangerous Pitfalls of Professional Leadership

All too frequently in Scripture we see chosen and blessed luminaries fall to the ground after success leads them to take matters into their own hands. This attitude of pride extends from Saul even to the New Testament case of a young missionary named Demas (see 1 Sam. 15:23; 2 Tim. 4:10).

Here in Judges we see it in the case of Gideon. The calloused attitude of a warrior engulfed the once humble and timid farmer. Judges 8:1-21 records a vicious, merciless pursuit that was carried out by Gideon and his men. Had they not won the battle? Had they not earned the right to command the surrounding inhabitants as they wished? If anyone stood in the way, he would be knocked flat–as were the Midianites.

The humble dependence of young Gideon turned, in one battle, into a frightening autocracy. Perhaps we may forgive his attitude in the bitterness of war and upon learning of the death of his family (see Judges 8:19). But there is surely a lesson here regarding how one can grow so professional and authoritarian in a leadership position that he loses his sensitivity to those around him.

Gideon leaned another lesson here. Leadership is hardly ever project-oriented; that is, the Midianite battle was not an *ad hoc* event. Now Gideon was expected to conquer Zebah and Zalmunna, and who knew what might be next? But certainly the greatest of Gideon's mistakes as a veteran leader (one became a veteran very quickly in those leaderless days) was his incomplete devotion to God. Almost in the same breath, as the old cliché suggests, Gideon told the people that the Lord would rule over them and that he had no aspirations to a kingship, and then he requested their gold in order to make a symbolical tribute to his house—a golden ephod. At best, the ephod was a compromise with worship of the true God.

So the land had peace 40 years in the days of Gideon—largely, I suppose, because of his control over the divisive tribes, thus presenting a unified defense to enemies without. But it is a sad tribute that what earlier appeared to be a beautiful model of leadership ended with a golden ephod causing Israel to sin (see Judges 8:27). It is interesting to note that the same phrase used in verse 27 appears in verse 33. In the days of Gideon, the people "went . . . a whoring" after Gideon's fabricated place of worship. After his death, they once again "went a whoring" after Baal.

What a curse that any man of God should so construct his leadership that the people who follow him carry an unhealthy reverence toward his person and work! This reverence could even, in small but important ways, supercede and controvert their reverence for God.

Deborah: The Leader Is a Lady

It is not uncommon in the pages of Scripture to see a woman elevated to a position of leadership. One could speak of Miriam or Esther in the Old Testament, and certainly Priscilla in the New Testament. But probably no woman in biblical history ever rose to the political heights of a man's world as did Deborah, the judge and prophetess. It is of no small tribute that she is the only woman mentioned in Rudolf Kittel's, *Great Men and Movements in Israel.* (KTAV.)

It has been loudly proclaimed by some that biblical Christianity discriminates against women. It has been alleged that the Apostle Paul, for example, was the outstanding male chauvinist of all time. Such statements are based on an unfortunate misunderstanding of Scripture and of the whole role of women in Christianity. As a matter of fact, the Bible clearly teaches a high status for women, and the role of women has risen significantly wherever the Gospel has gone. The history of modern missions alone is a sufficient attestation to what Christianity has to say about the status of women.

What is most specifically misunderstood is the difference between essence and function. The Bible teaches that there is no difference, in essence, between men and women. However, it does say that there is a difference of function between men and women in society, and most particularly between husbands and wives in the home. The Bible does not condemn the equality of men and women; rather, it sustains and establishes equality. However, it most certainly condemns the breaking down of distinctions marking the sexes—that is, the repudiation of biblical roles of men and women in the family, the church, and the larger society.

Accepting the biblical teaching of different roles for men and women, we may ask how a woman's leadership is to be understood. We must look at Scripture to see how the leadership of a woman among God's people is possible. It is a tribute to Deborah that her example identifies the different function of leadership which is given to women.

What we see so many times *by example* in the Old Testament, we also see *by principle* in the writings of Paul—notably his reminders to the young church leader, Timothy. Leadership in the office of elder and deacon, we learn in 1 Timothy 3, is to be limited to men who have certain qualifications. This passage does not teach the inferiority of women; it merely indicates how God expects the church to function in worship. How did Deborah exemplify female leadership in the early history of the Old Testament?

She Was Duly Appointed to Leadership

Deborah was unlike much of what we see in the extremes of our day—the hesitant wallflowers who refuse to become involved in public affairs, and the brazen and loquacious feminists who usurp every leadership position in sight. Deborah was the selection of God and her people for a post of leadership (see Judges 4:4). Edith Deen, depending largely upon Josephus and other traditional sources, suggests that

Deborah's leadership (like *all* good leadership) began at home:

> Long before Deborah became a leader in war, she was a homemaker. Her house was on the road between Ramah and Beth-el, in the hill country of Ephraim, where flourished olive and palm trees. It was under one of the royal date palms where she would sit and give counsel to the people who came to her.[1]

Deborah was not a career girl executive. Indeed, it is interesting that most of the women presented as leaders in Scripture are associated with a family setting. Esther came into leadership as the wife of a king. Priscilla is hardly identified apart from Aquila, although it may very well be that she was the most significant scholar and leader of the two. And Deborah, we learn, was the wife of Lapidoth, an obscure Hebrew man whose only introduction into history was through the leadership of his wife.

I do not mean to imply that single women cannot be leaders, because in our day this may be the more common pattern. However, I do think it is worth noticing that Scripture places a great deal of emphasis on family settings. It is apparently God's design that the most rewarding and definitive role for a woman is in the family setting (see 1 Tim. 5:14-15), but this relationship does not in any way hinder leadership. In Deborah's case, it may very well have advanced her work.

God had seen fit to give Deborah the gift of prophecy. In the Old Testament, this meant predicting future events—which is precisely what she did in her initial message to Barak (see Judges 4:6-7). We should not be astonished at this, for we know that even in the New Testament women were given the gift of prophecy. Philip's daughters exercised the gift in illuminating and expounding the truth of God in the days of the early church (see Acts 21:9).

She Worked Effectively in an Encouraging Role with Her Male Colleagues

It is quite apparent throughout the text that Deborah was the guiding light and sustaining spirit of the victory over Sisera and his armies (see Judges 4:6-9, 14). Nevertheless, she did not bypass Barak's proper role; rather, she asked him to call together the armies of Israel.

Apparently, Deborah's very presence would stimulate morale among the troops—so Barak requested her to make the journey to the battlefront. She agreed, and became an ancient Joan of Arc, symbolizing God's presence in His chosen leader right in the thick of battle.

Nevertheless, Deborah had to remind Barak that the glory would be neither his nor hers. God would take to Himself the glory for the battle.

The phrase "for the Lord shall sell Sisera into the hand of a woman" (Judges 4:9), seems at first to be a self-exalting statement on Deborah's part. But if we view it in the light of the song of Deborah, we can see that she may very well have been prophesying Sisera's death at the hand of Jael (see 5:24-31). The song gives a much greater portion of tribute to Jael than to Deborah, though the act of killing Sisera was more symbolic than military in its consequence.

I find it important, too, that Deborah took a constantly encouraging role with Barak. It does not take away from Barak's personal courage when we see that Deborah constantly reinforced his role (see Judges 4:14). Rather, it is a positive commentary on the status and impact of a spiritual woman whom God chose to use in a mighty way at a critical point in the history of His people.

Isn't it interesting that when God lists the heroes of the Old Testament in an honor roll of faith, Barak is included, but Deborah is not (see Heb. 11:32)? Somehow I feel that Deborah would have wanted it that way, since she seemed to understand clearly the difference in function between a man and a woman.

However, Deborah was certainly not slighted; the account in Judges 4-5 clearly identifies Deborah as the heroine of the victory over the Canaanites. Barak is not presented as the hero.

In one scholarly text, Deborah is described in the spirit of the biblical text:

> On the coins of the Roman Empire, Judaea is represented as a woman seated under a palm tree, captive and weeping. It is the contrast of that figure which will place before us the character and call of Deborah. It is the same Judaean palm, under whose shadow she sits, but not with downcast eyes, and folded hands, and extinguished hopes; with all the fire of faith and energy, eager for the battle, confident of the victory, strength of character, intellect, clearsightedness, tact and a wisdom which He alone who had called her to that lofty position could give—these were the endowments of Deborah, and she bravely did her best with them for the problems and the duties of that terrible time. The people must be roused to meet and conquer Sisera. It was the will of God. So she sent for the man whose duty it was to summon the fighting men to action, Barak, the son of Abinoam, and reiterated to him the command of God, and His instructions for the arrangement of the battle.[2]

She Was a Woman Who Knew How to Worship

The song of Deborah and Barak seems to have been composed and sung by both leaders. It is a duet of historical and theological dimensions which demonstrates, first of all, that Deborah understood the history of her people and had therefore been called to leadership from a background of that kind of intellectual resource.

One of the things I have always considered tragic is to see a young lady whose educational potential is extremely bright drop out of school in her freshman or sophomore year of college in order to go to work so that her newly acquired husband, perhaps a mediocre student, may finish his baccalaureate education. It is only a tribute to the primitive designs which remain in our modern society that such a pattern persists.

But the most remarkable thing about Deborah's victory ode is its character of worship. Hastings remarks:

> It is a strange thing that in the same soul there should throb delight in battle, the almost delight in murder, and these lofty thoughts. But let us learn the lesson that true love to God means hatred of God's enemy.[3]

The battle was the Lord's. He was to be praised. His people had been delivered by a power given to leaders whom He had chosen and equipped. Deborah sought only to rejoice as "a mother in Israel" about God's unique way of delivering the pagan general into the hands of a woman (Judges 5:7).

And the song ends on a beautiful note: "So let all thine enemies perish, O Lord: but let them that love him be as the sun when he goeth forth in his might. And the land had rest forty years" (Judges 5:31).

That was, of course, what Deborah had wanted all along. The battle was only a means to an end, a necessary evil to achieve peace in the land. Now she could go back to her palm tree between Ramah and Beth-el and continue again with the task so close to her heart—counseling and judging her people.

Rudolf Kittel, that outstanding Old Testament scholar, wrote this final paragraph in his chapter on Deborah:

> Deborah, who has much in common with Joan of Arc, had one advantage over her. The latter had first to be burned at the stake to become a saint. In her very lifetime Deborah had the honor of being called a "mother in Israel."[4]

Saul: Looks Aren't Everything

In leadership studies, there is an expression used to describe the kind of individual who, because of his appearance, seems to be a leader to everyone who sees him. They call him a "mythical leader," an idea which comes from the myth that leadership can be defined on the bases of height, color of eyes, or volume of voice, rather than the realistic components of contribution to group goals and ability to handle a given situation.

Saul was not really a mythical leader—because he was duly appointed by God to his post. But it is apparent that people admired him physically (see 1 Sam. 9:2).

He entered the picture in approximately 1 Samuel 9 as God's answer to His people's request for a king. The request was probably motivated by several factors. There was the failure of Samuel's sons to follow in the spiritual leadership of their father (see 1 Sam. 8:1-5). Add the continuing Philistine threat and the people's desire to be like other nations.

Humility When Chosen

When Samuel began to inform Saul of the magnificent future ahead of him, the young man responded: "Am I not a Benjamite, of the smallest of the tribes of Israel, and my family the least of all the families of the tribe of Benjamin? Why then do you speak to me in this way?" (1 Sam. 9:21 NASB). When he got back to his family, he told about his visit to the seer but did not mention the kingship (10:16). Later, at the inauguration party called by Samuel, Saul was found hiding in the baggage. Apparently he was shy and hesitant about taking the leadership role.

There are both positive and negative lessons here. It is, without doubt, a biblical attitude to be humble not only at the time of selection for leadership, but also throughout all the months and years one holds a leadership position in the service for Christ. But humility is not synonymous with running away from responsibility or with merely being shy. Saul's humility was commendable here, but it was also commendable that he soon shook off his provincial fear of people and faced up to the responsibilities God had put before him.

Sometimes a seeming humility can be just an excuse for an unwillingness to take responsibility. This does not seem to be so in Saul's case, but we must always be careful that such an improper substitution does not trip us up.

A Changed Heart for Leadership

The shyness and hesitancy which seemed to characterize Saul's personality throughout his life up to this point disappeared as God gave him a new heart. The words of Samuel confirm that the new heart was linked inseparably to the leadership responsibility, a connection which was, doubtless, God's intent: "Then the Spirit of the Lord will come upon you mightily, and you shall prophesy with them and be changed into another man. And it shall be when these signs come to you, do for yourself what the occasion requires; for God is with you" (1 Sam. 10:6-7 NASB).

What a wonderful promise for leadership! How many times those of us who hold various positions of responsibility have bowed before the Lord to request the kind of wisdom necessary to carry out those responsibilities! Saul could no longer spend time wandering around the country looking for lost animals. He had been catapulted by the sovereign plan of God into the leadership of his nation.

Unlike Moses and Joshua, he did not spend 40 years preparing for the task. Unlike Joseph, he did not have the backing of a wealthy nation and a reigning monarch. He now occupied the office "where the buck stops," and only the constant attention of the Spirit of God could maintain him in a position of dynamic leadership.

Failure to Obey the Lord

Scarcely had King Saul begun his reign when he stumbled and headed on a downward path. The king's primary and constant sin was disobedience to God. Early victories at Jabesh-gilead and Michmash apparently developed in him an unhealthy self-confidence which quickly ballooned into pride. In 1 Samuel 13, King Saul waited for Samuel at Gilgal and then impatiently offered a burnt sacrifice when the aging priest did not arrive just when the king thought he should. Such conduct was a violation of basic Old Testament law. Samuel's response was immediate and devastating:

> You have acted foolishly; you have not kept the commandment of the Lord your God, which He commanded you, for now the Lord would have established your kingdom over Israel forever. But now your kingdom shall not endure. The Lord has sought out for Himself a man after His own heart, and the Lord has appointed him as ruler over His people, because you have not kept what the Lord commanded you (1 Sam. 13:13-14 NASB).

A second act of disobedience is recorded in 1 Samuel 15, when the king was commanded to completely destroy every living thing among the Amalekites after his victory. The reason for that was the symbolic renouncing on the part of

Israel of any personal gain from the victory—it was purely the work of God. But once again Saul did what he thought was right rather than what God had commanded—and then lied about the situation (15:13). He blamed the people and refused to take the responsibility himself. On this occasion, Samuel verbalized a marvelous principle of godly living: "... to obey is better than sacrifice, and to hearken than the fat of rams" (15:22). The ultimate rejection of Saul by Jehovah was now complete. From this point on, Saul merely lived out his term as a spiritual lame duck.

Foolish and Hasty Judgments

There is no question but that Saul suffered from some kind of emotional or psychological illness during his declining days. How much of it was purely spiritual and how much an actual health problem, we cannot diagnose. But it is evident that this deficiency—spiritual, emotional, mental, or all three—caused Saul to demonstrate fatal deficiencies in judgment.

On one occasion, he pronounced a curse on anyone who ate before he had taken full revenge on his enemies (see 1 Sam. 14:24). So Saul led a half-starved army into battle. The result was that the troops, in their hunger, tore into the bloody meat of butchered animals taken in battle (v. 32). The king was forced to retract his command. Saul would have killed his own son, Jonathan, a hero of the day's warfare, if he had not been stopped by the people themselves (v. 45). Apparently the army had already lost faith in the decision-making power of their commander.

Jealousy of Subordinates

The Scriptures reveal Saul to have been a leader who tried to hurt those who wanted to help him. Saul admired young David and loved him (see 1 Sam. 16:21). However, as soon as the young leader began to exert his own gifts of leadership, Saul felt threatened. The king's love turned to hate, and his respect turned to anger. A jealous, tormented spirit possessed the declining king, whose defensive insecurity became more than he could bear. Saul carried with him to the grave the fear that this young warrior was aggressively attempting to usurp his throne.

How important it is that those of us who are leaders exercise the godly responsibility of developing other leaders! A Sunday school superintendent must not be jealous of his departmental superintendents, but must seek to elevate their responsibility and encourage their initiative. A pastor should not feel threatened by the vibrant ministry of his associates, but should rather thank God for the use of their gifts in the church. This is not an easy outlook to have, but a leader *can* have it if the grace of God is working in him. Moses evidently did not feel threatened by Joshua, for example. As leaders, we should have the attitude of John the Baptist toward Jesus: "He must increase, but I must decrease" (John 3:30). Here is a classic model for leadership in all times and seasons.

Seeking Counsel from God's Enemies

On occasion, Saul showed momentary flashes of repentance, but never anything that really lasted. Toward the close of his life, he desperately sought some message from the dead prophet, Samuel, whom he sorely missed. The enormous vacuum created by the absence of this godly prophet only increased the spiritual decline of the king.

Saul took a final step toward spiritual degradation by visiting the medium at En-dor (see 1 Sam. 28:7-25). This was in violation of his own order and was another attempt at deceit. The king had already tried to get guidance from the Lord, but he was too late—for God wouldn't respond to his inquries (28:5-6). So Saul violated every principle of Old Testament godliness, and attempted to use the power of evil spirits.

The fact that Samuel appeared to Saul and spoke to him was not due to the woman's power. As a matter of fact, no one was more surprised than she when the prophet appeared.

Saul got a divine message as he had desired, but the content certainly was not what he wanted. Samuel told Saul one more time that God had rejected him because of his disobedience. The Israelite army would be routed by the Philistines the next day, and Saul and his sons would die.

The respect of the Philistines for Saul's military ability explains why they fastened his body to the walls of Beth-shan (see 1 Sam. 31:10). They felt, no doubt, that they finally were rid of this giant of a man who had plagued them on numerous occasions in recent years. However, the faithful men of Jabesh-gilead remembered how the young king had rescued them from the Amorites; so, at the risk of their own lives, they removed the bodies of Saul and his sons from the walls of Beth-shan and brought them home for burning and burial in Jabesh.

The close of Saul's life was not happy, and his death was not pleasant. But the sacred record provides ample lessons. Leadership is definied by spiritual gifts, the call of God, one's relationship to his group, and one's ability to take responsibility in certain situations. Divine evaluation is not primarily based on size or volume. Apparently in God's scale of values, obedience and faithfulness are worth considerably more than a striking outward appearance.

David: Human Relations Expert

Because leadership is invariably bound up in working with people, the concept of human relations is extremely important in any leadership role. The team leader sets the tone for the team spirit. The presence which he displays in the organization is of extreme importance to the way each individual responds to his task and how he views his role in the larger scheme.

David had no formal training in management practice, but he certainly seems to have had a unique gift of administration. He responded with a positive sense of human relations in all aspects of his leadership. From his obedience in the house of Jesse to the dynamic of his aging presence on the throne, his sensitivity and concern for people were remarkable. Let us trace some of the basic patterns of human relations which David demonstrated.

Human Relations with Peers

The friendship between David and Jonathan is one of the

most beautiful stories in the Old Testament. In the exact sense, however, David and Jonathan were not peers. Indeed, Jonathan perceived that they were rivals for the throne. But their love for each other overcame what could have been a nasty situation. Had God not indicated His choice of David as the next king, one could well imagine the ex-shepherd as Jonathan's number one supporter for the post.

Too often when we think of human relations in leadership we think only of the leader's relation to subordinates. But it is extremely important to keep parallel peer relations in order. Of course, after David became king, he had no peer.

After the clandestine meeting on the archery field, Jonathan said to his friend, "The Lord will be between me and you, and between my descendants and your descendants forever" (1 Sam. 20:42 NASB). At this point, Jonathan was a prince—and therefore held a position superior to David. But it is apparent that these young men thought of each other as peers. They exercised the suggestion of Paul to the Philippian church—to think of others as more important than oneself (see Phil. 2:1-4).

Human Relations with a Superior

The sterling quality of David's character never showed its brilliance better than during the dark days when he was on the run from King Saul. On at least two occasions, he had the opportunity to kill the king (see 1 Sam. 24, 26). But it never occurred to him to do that. His respect for and faithfulness to Saul were evident, though the king certainly was doing nothing to earn such an attitude.

There is a marvelous lesson here for those who feel their superiors are acting unjustly toward them. In many instances, as in this one, the analysis may be true. In general employment or church ministry, it may very well be that the person who is responsible for supervising your work has not been fair with you. What, then, is the proper biblical response?

Look at the example of David. He said to Saul:

> May the Lord judge between you and me, and may the Lord avenge me on you; but my hand shall not be against you. As the proverb of the ancients says, "Out of the wicked comes forth wickedness"; but my hand shall not be against you. After whom has the king of Israel come out? Whom are you pursuing? A dead dog, a single flea? The Lord therefore be judge and decide between you and me; and may He see and plead my cause, and deliver me from your hand (1 Sam. 24:12-15 NASB).

It is never proper for a Christian to usurp authority or to attempt to unseat those who have been placed over him. So behave the kings of the Gentiles; this is not worthy of the child of God. Rather, one is to be in submission and keep his own heart right before God, leaving the results to Him.

Human Relations with the General Staff

David's leadership was primarily military, and his general staff was, therefore, the officers and men of his army. Scripture gives various glimpses of what David thought about these men and how they responded to his leadership.

For example, after the defeat of the Amalekites, some of the less gracious of David's men were against giving any of the loot to those who guarded their camp. But David's response echoed with characteristic kindness: "You must not do so, my brothers, with what the Lord has given us, who has kept us. . . . And who will listen to you in this matter? For as his share is who goes down to the battle, so shall his share be who stays by the baggage; they shall share alike" (1 Sam. 30:23-24 NASB).

It is often characteristic of the men in the front lines to think and speak negatively of their officers, who sometimes seem to give all the orders and do none of the fighting. But David was held in the highest respect by his troops. On one occasion, he planned to lead the army himself against the rebellious troops of Israel. His men would not hear of the plan, and said: "You should not go out; for if we indeed flee, they will not care about us, even if half of us die, they will not care about us. But you are worth ten thousand of us; therefore now it is better that you be ready to help us from the city" (2 Sam. 18:3 NASB). What pastor or Sunday school superintendent would not like to hear his people praise him this way!

It could hardly be said that David introduced democratic leadership into the military monarchy of ancient, theocratic Israel; but he certainly did demonstrate a skill in staff relations which was far ahead of its time. William Sanford LaSor writes:

> The organization of David's kingdom, which is described largely in 1 Chronicles 22-27, is very interesting. It gives us a good insight into the mind of the man. He apparently realized that the kingdom was not to be built on the personality of the king alone, but on an organization of men around him. He seems to have taken many of his ideas from the Egyptians, but whether he got them directly, or through his knowledge of the Philistines (you remember that in the days when he was an outlaw he had lived with the Philistines), we do not know. The organizational structure of his kingdom was a sort of pyramid. It had a broad base and narrowed toward the top, where there was just one man as king.[1]

Human Relations with a Subordinate

There are a number of persons who could be selected to exemplify David's relations with a subordinate, but certainly no one fills the bill better than Joab, the commander in chief of his army. Joab is a complex character who at times borders on genuine sympathy and sensitivity–and at others seems like a mercenary butcher.

This was not at all unlike David's own personality–which fact may account for the king's constant willingness to put up with Joab. It was Joab who convinced David to bring Absalom back to Jerusalem (see 2 Sam. 14). It was Joab, again, who warned David to trust in God and not in the vast numbers of his own nation (see 2 Sam. 24:1-10).

But it was also Joab who mercilessly murdered Absalom against the king's command (see 2 Sam. 18:14-17). It was Joab who butchered Amasa, his political rival for the headship of the army (see 2 Sam. 20:7-11).

Long before Peter Drucker wrote *The Effective Executive* (Harper and Row), King David understood one of the basic tenets of that book: In relating to your subordinates, emphasize their strengths. Joab had many weaknesses, but he was a good soldier and a winning commander. Just as Abraham Lincoln put up with Grant's drinking because Grant knew how to win battles, David put up with Joab's ruthlessness.

Ultimately, however, justice must be done; and David said to Solomon: "You also know what Joab . . . did . . . to Abner . . . and to Amasa . . . whom he killed; he also shed the blood of war in peace. . . . So act according to your wisdom, and do not let his gray hair go down to Sheol in peace" (1 Kings 2:5-6 NASB).

A blend of justice and grace is not only the pattern of David regarding Joab—and the pattern of God with man generally—but it is also a wise model for every leader in subordinate relations.

There is a great deal more in the story of David, of course, but it does not pertain to the specific leadership lessons we seek in these selected passages. We could speak about his failure as a father and his success as a hymn writer. We could talk about his lustful sin or his love for God. The complex character of this man is virtually a lifetime study. James Montgomery Boice says it well in a little book entitled, *How God Can Use Nobodies:*

> David's own poetry has come down to us through his psalms. Many persons who do not know a word spoken by George Washington or Abraham Lincoln are steeped in these verses. Through many of the psalms, David emerges as a prophet of the coming Messiah; and Christians can never forget that it was through David's royal and legal line that Jesus, the Messiah, entered history that wonderful day nearly two thousand years ago.[2]

Solomon: Facing That Building Program

9

Solomon is one of the most illustrious characters in the pages of the Old Testament. Scripture is completely silent on his childhood—a rather unusual fact in view of what we learn about David's *other* sons. After he was catapulted into the kingship, however, he immediately responded to the vastness of the task by demonstrating a sensitivity to the requirements of leadership. There appeared to be no question in David's mind that this was God's choice in the succession of the kingship; Solomon seemed quite content to shoulder the staggering responsibilities.

The scriptural record first describes Solomon's marriage with the daughter of Pharaoh. Doubtless this was a political move to ally Israel with the great neighboring kingdom of Egypt. That Solomon was able to accomplish such a union is evidence of the position and influence of the Israelite kingdom in the Mediterranean world of his day.

But we should not picture the wealth and influence of Solomon as being complete in those early days. It was the blessing of God upon Solomon's reign which produced the bounteous wealth we associate with his leadership. To be sure, the vast gains in land brought about by David's military kingdom were impressive. But as Alfred Edersheim clearly puts it:

> The conquests so lately made had not yet been consolidated; the means at the king's disposal were still comparatively scanty; tribal jealousies were scarcely appeased; and Solomon himself was young and wholly inexperienced. Any false step might prove fatal; even want of some brilliant success might disintegrate what was but imperfectly welded together.[1]

Perhaps the most significant event of the leadership of Solomon was the extensive–indeed, incredible–building program which characterized his reign. It is to this aspect of his leadership that we direct our attention.

Most leaders in top positions find themselves faced, sooner or later, with a building program. Although few modern building programs begin to equal Solomon's temple and palace, much can yet be learned from his example in organization and leadership. Let us take a look at some of the characteristics which made Solomon a master leader in building.

Solomon Knew the Primary Requisite of Leadership

Solomon was not a great theologian like his father; although his proverbs demonstrate a high sensitivity to the nature and laws of God, he does not seem to have equaled the spiritual depth of David. Yet when it came time to answer God's strategic challenge, "Ask what I shall give thee" (1 Kings 3:5), Solomon had the only correct response: "Give . . . thy servant an understanding heart to judge thy people, that I may discern between good and bad: for who is able to judge this thy so great a people?" (1 Kings 3:9).

Anyone who has served in a place of strategic leadership emphathizes with Solomon's request. How comforting is the New Testament injunction from the pen of James: "If any of you lack wisdom, let him ask of God, . . . and it shall be given him" (James 1:5). At this early point in his leadership, Solomon had no way of knowing what kinds of problems and complexities lay in the future. But he had already seen the impossibility of exercising leadership without the constant control of the wisdom of God.

It is typical of God to respond with more than what His people ask. Solomon had not asked to be the wisest man who ever lived, but that's what God made him. Solomon did not ask for riches and honor, but God gave them to him in a bounteous measure. Solomon prospered because he was a leader who knew how to put first things first.

Solomon Had the Advantage of a Peaceful Administration

Solomon was a fine administrator. William Sanford LaSor calls him an "internationalist" who expanded the provincial kingdom of David across much of the known world of that day. Certainly we must attribute some of the peacefulness of the kingdom to Solomon's wise administration. But let us not forget that there was a unique blessing of God in conjunction with Solomon's reign—and that much of what Jehovah did for Solomon, He did in memory of the righteousness of David. Nevertheless, the unique division of the government into 12 administrative districts—each of which was required to support the court for one month of the year—was a demonstration of the kind of organization that Solomon carried out.

Any administrator knows he cannot give his attention to constructive matters until the destructive problems around him have been settled. God forbade David to build the temple personally (because of his bloody war record) and conferred the honor of the actual construction on his son; but there is some doubt whether David would have had any time for temple-building even if his attempt *had* been sanctioned. He was too busy putting out political fires, large and small. The administrator who is constantly faced with meeting the budget will have difficulty in giving his attention to a long-range building program. The leader who is regularly engaged in squabbles with members of his staff is in no position to give himself unreservedly to the constructive aspect of leadership.

Solomon Recognized the Necessity for Professional Help

The most important thing a leader can do is surround himself with high-level staff officers who are experts in their fields. The chief executive is, by virtue of his task, a generalist. True, he probably came up through the ranks by specializing in one area. For example, a college president is often drawn from the deanship, and is thereby familiar with the academic side of the institution. But as soon as he assumes the presidency, he is besieged by a variety of issues with which he may not have had much experience. He must be able to choose men who can provide the kind of expertise necessary to form and sustain a competent administration.

That is exactly what Solomon did in both his building and naval programs. *The National Geographic* for August 1974 carried an excellent article on the Phoenicians and mentioned their assisting Solomon in his building task:

> "Behold, I purpose to build an house unto the name of the Lord my God," declared the Hebrews' King Solomon (1 Kings 5:5). But his people–former nomads–lacked experience with monumental architecture, so he turned to an ally, the master builder, King Hiram of Tyre. During the next seven years the Phoenician-style temple rose in Jerusalem, as legions of workmen, countless loads of finely cut stone, cedar and other timbers, and draperies of purple linen poured in. A renowned Tyrian metalworker cast two great pillars of bronze for the entrance.[2]

Solomon's Building Project Had the Blessing of God

We may assume that Solomon was led by God to begin the actual building of the temple. Verbal permission had already been given to David, as far as the idea of the project was concerned; the great warrior-king had begun to gather plans and materials, as well as arrange the liturgical service for the temple. God's only restriction was that David's son—not David himself—would be involved in the actual construction.

The point is that this massive building program was not carried out at the whim of some Oriental monarch. Toward the end of the construction time, Jehovah reminded Solomon again: "Concerning this house which thou art in building, if thou wilt walk in my statutes, and execute my judgments, and keep all my commandments to walk in them; then will I perform my word with thee, which I spake unto David thy father: and I will dwell among the children of Israel, and will not forsake my people Israel" (1 Kings 6:12-13).

The necessity for seeking the mind of God before beginning any significant building project is as important in our day as it was in Solomon's. LaSor estimates the total cost of Solomon's building projects at about 4.4 billion dollars—a staggering sum for a small monarchy.

But Solomon advanced the work confidently, knowing that God was with him. The same principle applies in our own day. The task can be done and the building constructed, if the Christian leader is confident that he walks within the will of God in carrying out the enormous task of building.

Solomon Did Not Quit until the Work Was Finished

It is interesting to see this phrase appearing and reappearing in the text of 1 Kings: "So he built the house, and finished it" (6:9, see also vv. 14, 38). So often church building programs stop short of completion. In an effort to save a sum (which often represents less than five percent of the total building cost), we plan to leave floors untiled, walls unpainted, windows undraped, doors unhung, and so forth.

The idea seems to be that professional contractors can finish the general construction of the building, while the congregation takes care of minor details in a series of Saturday "workdays." Sometimes that practice actually succeeds; more often, a church building in which people have invested thousands of dollars remains unfinished and unattractive for months. It would be far better to follow Solomon's example and finish the job.

I wish we could end the story of Solomon with his prayer of dedication at the temple, which is recorded in chapter 8 of 1 Kings. From that point on, however, his story is one of perversion of wealth and straying from God. Scarcely nine and a half chapters of Scripture are given to the description of this great reign—a pittance compared to how the story of David is treated.

Nevertheless, though we may not find spiritual living and lifetime dedication in the reign of Solomon, we do learn a unique lesson of leadership in his development of one of the greatest building programs in history. Nor should we forget that at several points in the New Testament God likens the church to a building. A pastor or Sunday school superintendent is therefore involved in a "building" program all the time. Surely the principles used in physical building apply as well to the construction of God's spiritual house through preaching and teaching His Word.

Ezekiel: With What, Lord?

Ezekiel began his prophetic ministry in the year 593 B.C., the fifth year of the captivity of King Jehoiachin. The young man had been deported to Babylon in 597; he was to lose his wife nine years later on the first day of the siege of Jerusalem. Ezekiel was both a priest and the son of a priest, but he did not begin his prophetic ministry until after he was carried to Babylon in the Captivity.

The general theme of Ezekiel's writing seems to be one of comfort and exhortation. Jeremiah predicted the destruction of Jerusalem and poured out woes upon God's people because of their disobedience and idolatry. Much of the same thing occurs in the early chapters of the Book of Ezekiel; but while he issues God's message of warning to those still living in Jerusalem, he speaks with gentleness to the captives "by the river Chebar" (Ezek. 1:3). Merrill F. Unger picks up a key phrase which identifies the thrust of Ezekiel's writings:

> The phrase "they shall know that I am God" occurs more than thirty times in the book from 6:7 through 39:28. This repeated

declaration that their punishments would bring about this happy result was amply fulfilled. The Babylonian captivity cured the Jews of idolatry. Up to that time, despite everything, they continually fell into idolatry. From that day forward, however, whatever sins the Jews had been guilty of they have not been idolaters.[1]

God's Truth for a People with Need

In the time of Ezekiel, there was a leadership vacuum much like the one which existed in the days of the judges. From his position as a captive in Babylon, Ezekiel could do little but warn the remainder of Jews in the land, who had not yet been brought in captivity. There was a leadership vacuum there, too. But to his own generation, Ezekiel could bring both warning and comfort, constantly reminding them of the sins which had brought the people to Babylon and sustaining their faith in Jehovah by promises of ultimate national restoration.

In Ezekiel 2, we find the prophet responding to commands of Jehovah, much in the way that many leaders have in the early days of their call. Actually, Ezekiel did not dialogue with God in this chapter; but we can infer, from what the Lord says to the young prophet, something of the feelings of inadequacy which gripped him at this crucial moment.

> And he said unto me, Son of man, stand upon thy feet, and I will speak unto thee. And the spirit entered into me when he spake unto me, and set me upon my feet, that I heard him that spake unto me. And he said unto me, Son of man, I send thee to the children of Israel, to a rebellious nation that hath rebelled against me: they and their fathers have transgressed against me, even unto this very day. For they are impudent children and stiffhearted. I do send thee unto them; and thou shalt say unto them, Thus saith the Lord God. And they, whether they will hear, or whether they will forbear, (for they are a rebellious house,) yet shall know that there hath been a prophet among them" (Ezek. 2:1-5).

The rebellion had not yet cooled in the hearts of Ezekiel's people, even though they were exiles and captives. Several times in this short chapter, Jehovah reminded Ezekiel that he would be facing a people who did not want to hear his message; therefore, any resources he could bring to the task would be essential. The Lord proceeded to identify a primary resource when He showed Ezekiel one of the many heavenly visions which that prophet was privileged to have.

The vision of the scroll was then spread before Ezekiel. Along with it were these words from God: "Son of man, eat that thou findest, eat this roll, and go speak unto the house of Israel" (Ezek. 3:1). We must understand, of course, that the word "roll" refers to an unrolled scroll, and not some edible form of bread. The whole vision is symbolic in that God was telling Ezekiel that he must internalize His truth before he is ready to minister to other people.

This is certainly no new emphasis in Scripture. We see it in the lives of Moses, Joshua, and others. Ezekiel's people were rebellious, but very needy. Their gruff exterior was only a veneer covering the desperate state of their hearts. But until Ezekiel had something to say–until he had internalized God's truth–he was not ready to minister to them.

Family and church leaders must fill much the same need as Ezekiel did. How futile–indeed, how dishonest–to stand before a Sunday school class without first having internalized the Word of God. Notice also that Ezekiel did not abhor God's truth as he ate it. It was in his mouth "as honey for sweetness" (Ezek. 3:3). What a beautiful thing to be said about a person's response to God's truth!

God's Call in the Hours of Uncertainty

As chapter 3 develops, we continue to learn how strongly God wants Ezekiel to understand his call. The message from heaven repeats the theme that Ezekiel was not sent to some exotic foreign mission field, but to his own people. This was not Ezekiel's choice; it was God's. I imagine the one thing that sustained Ezekiel during those dark hours of rejection and the distortion of his message by his own people was the recognition that God had called him and that God would therefore sustain him in the task.

> And he said unto me, Son of man, go, get thee unto the house of Israel, and speak with my words unto them. For thou art not sent to a people of a strange speech and of an hard language, but to the house of Israel; not to many people of a strange speech and of an hard language, whose words thou canst not understand. Surely, had I sent thee to them, they would have hearkened unto thee" (Ezek. 3:4-6).

Again, here is a very important lesson for church workers. At times, when those hours of uncertainty come, it is important to remember that we serve in our ministries not because of the request of a pastor or a Sunday school superintendent, but because the hand of God has singled us out for those positions.

God's Model in an Age of Confusion

One of the characteristics of leadership in all ages has been the responsibility of example. In Christian leadership, the leader looks to the Lord for the primary demonstration of what he is to be; then he reflects that image to his followers.

In chapter 12 of the Book of Ezekiel, we see an interesting description of the prophet's behavior. Ezekiel was in the process of moving. He packed his baggage and moved it from one place to another in full view of all the people in his area. The key phrase is at the end of verse 6: "I have set thee for a sign unto the house of Israel." God wanted to demonstrate to His people in the Exile that they would be allowed to return. This message of hope and promise was designed to produce faith and optimism. Of course, Ezekiel did as he was commanded: "I brought forth my stuff by day, as stuff for captivity, and in the even I digged through the wall with mine hand; I brought it forth in the twilight, and I bare it upon my shoulder in their sight" (v. 7).

Sometimes, even today, leaders are called upon by God to do unusual things. These actions may be misunderstood by others. Frequently, the misunderstanding is due not so much to the leader's behavior as to the confusion and carnality of the age in which he lives. Because society has lost its moorings, because even God's people tend to be somewhat chaotic in their thinking about truth and error, because value systems may have dropped anchor in a sea of relativity, the demonstration of God's pattern must be maintained by the leader. This was not the only time Ezekiel served as a role model, of course, but the particular passage we stress demonstrates that component of leadership in his life and ministry.

God's Courage in a Task of Loneliness

Over 10 years ago, I prepared the text for a book which was published later under the title *Leadership for Church Education.* In that manuscript, I wrote the following paragraph:

> When the investment has been made, a return in the form of appreciation and thanks can be logically expected. Instead, there is often the offense of some who misunderstand and retaliate negatively for all of the efforts in their behalf. At moments like this the limelight dims, and the life of leadership becomes a life of loneliness.[2]

In the intervening time, I have experienced the reality of that paragraph on numerous occasions. You have, too, if you have been thrust by God into a role of leadership for any period of time. In those moments of loneliness, one must call upon God for courage to be sustained in the task. God said to Ezekiel on one occasion: "Son of man, eat thy bread with quaking, and drink thy water with trembling and with carefulness" (Ezek. 12:18). The word rendered "carefulness" in the King James Version actually means "anxiety." It reflects the unsettled situation in which Ezekiel found himself.

Certainly, Ezekiel experienced loneliness at the time of his wife's death. Note the following text from Ezekiel 24:

> The word of the Lord came unto me, saying, Son of man, behold, I take away from thee the desire of thine eyes with a

stroke: yet neither shalt thou mourn nor weep, neither shall thy tears run down. Forbear to cry, make no mourning for the dead, bind the tire of thine head upon thee, and put on thy shoes upon thy feet, and cover not thy lips, and eat not the bread of men. So I spake unto the people in the morning: and at even my wife died; and I did in the morning as I was commanded" (vv. 15-18).

God's Demand in the Role of Leadership

The famous "watchman" passage in Ezekiel appears in chapter 33. We frequently use it to emphasize the role of evangelism–and that kind of emphasis is not wrong. But in context the picture is much broader. Ezekiel stood between God and the people. He had the responsibility of hearing the message from the Lord and sharing it with the people. From that point on, it became their responsibility to hear and respond–or, if they chose, to hear and *not* respond. In either case, Ezekiel's task was finished, as to his continuing accountability.

However, until Ezekiel had stood in the gap–until he had responded to God's demand–he was still held responsible. God will not allow His leaders to shirk responsibility, even though they may frequently find that characteristic in their followers. The pressure is always there; the demands are always present. Ezekiel was to be a watchman unto the house of Israel.

What kind of watchman task has God given you? What responsibilities does He lay before you? What are the resources which He brings your way to enable you to carry out that task effectively? Ezekiel furnishes an example of a young man whom God had selected for leadership; he was thrust into a task which he did not ask for. In that task, he responded with great sensitivity to the provision God always makes for His leaders.

Daniel: Consistency Comes Out on Top

Probably because the story of Daniel is so familiar, we sometimes miss the thread of spiritual life woven so carefully through the narrative of the book. Here again we have a prophet writing about captivity, but in a considerably different position than that which we encountered when we studied the story of Ezekiel. Daniel was elevated from captive to counselor, from peasant to prime minister.

There are many points in the Book of Daniel which we could examine for leadership lessons; the one upon which this chapter focuses is the quiet consistency typifying Daniel's relationship with God. Everything Daniel did in public was possible because of what he had accomplished in private. He maintained a pipeline to heaven, and thus sustained his leadership role by drawing upon divine resources.

Childhood Training

We do not have any explicit information about Daniel's early life. However, from what we see of the early years of his captivity, we may assume that he was well stabilized in a life of godliness before he ever came to Babylon. As a matter of fact, such stability is reflected in many of the transplanted children of Bible history. It is observable in Daniel, in his companions, in the slave girl who served Naaman, in Joseph, and in other less notable Old Testament characters. The emphasis on family training, so important to Old Testament Jews, had built within these young people a conviction and a commitment that stood them in good stead during difficult years in foreign lands.

Conviction and Commitment

In Daniel 1:8 we see that the prophet had made up his mind not to accept the food and wine which the king offered to him and his colleagues. Why did Daniel make such a commitment? There was probably nothing specifically offensive about the food, although it certainly would not have been prepared according to Levitical procedures; Daniel's refusal to eat or drink derived from awareness of the issue at stake. He may very well have seen the intent of the king to turn the captives' minds from their fatherland and its God by the pleasures and physical delights of Babylon. Dr. Robert Culver comments on this passage:

> Had Daniel been one of the easy-going Christians of our day who is prepared to let any worldly pleasure or entertainment, earthly gain or excitement, be an excuse for setting aside the claims of the Lord upon them, we would never have heard of this firm choice of his. But then, we would never have heard of Daniel either! He certainly would never have adopted "safety first" as his slogan! What worldly people call squeamishness may be truly a matter of principle.[1]

Daniel's decision was accepted by his pagan captors, precisely because God willed it so and had already turned their minds in his favor. Daniel and his friends went on a vegetarian diet, and God honored their choice by strengthening them physically.

In a passage like this, there is certainly no intent on the part of Scripture to teach any particular diet for Christians. The central theme is not what Daniel did or did not eat or drink. Rather, the passage focuses attention on the conviction and commitment which enabled Daniel, even in the frustrating captivity of an alien nation, to stand firm for what he believed right.

Maximizing Divine Resources

In Daniel 1:17 we learn that God gave these four young men great ability to acquire knowledge and wisdom. They demonstrated an intellectual skill exceptional even among the Chaldeans, who were known as the brilliant scholars of that day. In addition, Daniel had an unusual ability to understand and interpret the meanings of dreams and visions. God had called Daniel to a special kind of leadership, and He had equipped him with the resources necessary to implement that leadership.

There are certainly people in positions of leadership to which they have not been called. In some of these cases, we see failure and frustration; one management expert has referred to this phenomenon as "the Peter principle"—which states that bureaucratic organizations always promote people to the level of their incompetence. For example, a person who may have been an adequate Sunday school teacher becomes, upon promotion, a mediocre departmental superintendent—and later, perhaps a very poor general Sunday school superintendent.

The Peter principle can never apply, however, to Christians who are called to certain positions of leadership. Surely Daniel would have been a prime candidate for incompetence in a task that required far more from him than he could ever have brought to it. But God gave him the resources for the task, and Daniel knew how to maximize those resources.

Notice the prayer that he offered in Daniel 2:20-23; here is the text from the New American Standard Bible:

Let the name of God be blessed forever and ever,
For wisdom and power belong to Him.
And it is He who changes the times and the epochs;
He removes kings and establishes kings;
He gives wisdom to wise men,
And knowledge to men of understanding.
It is He who reveals the profound and hidden things;
He knows what is in the darkness,
And the light dwells with Him.
To Thee, O God of my fathers, I give thanks and praise,
For Thou hast given me wisdom and power;
Even now Thou hast made known to me what we requested of Thee,
For Thou hast made known to us the king's matter.

Ezekiel 14:14 and 20 also bear witness to Daniel's righteousness and compare him with Noah and Job. Another passage in the same book refers to his wisdom (see Ezek. 28:3). We must remember that Ezekiel was Daniel's contemporary, and that he had access to the kind of information which would enable him to describe Daniel accurately.

Humility and Honesty

One of the key verses for understanding the spiritual success of Daniel is the thirtieth verse of chapter 2. Although merely a parenthetical statement in his report to the king, it is quite important: "But as for me, this secret is not revealed to me for any wisdom that I have more than any living, but for their sakes that shall make known the interpretation to the king, and that thou mightest know the thoughts of thy heart."

It is striking to recognize that both Daniel and Nebuchadnezzar, the righteous servant and the pagan monarch, were minor actors in God's universal theater. He was using Nebuchadnezzar to form history, but He used Daniel to form Nebuchadnezzar. No one who reads the Book of Daniel carefully can doubt the authenticity of this doctrine of God's sovereignty.

How easy it is to take credit for leadership when matters are going well! Daniel knew that he had the answer to Nebuchadnezzar's dream; the prophet could have advanced himself significantly by grabbing whatever praise and honor were forthcoming. No doubt he could have secured these from Nebuchadnezzar, but in doing so he would have immediately lost favor with God. That Nebuchadnezzar elevated him anyhow is hardly to the point; Daniel could not have known in advance what the results of honest humility would be. Someone once aptly said that there is no limit to the good a man can do if he does not care who gets the credit.

Faithfulness in Prayer

One of the great spiritual lessons of the Book of Daniel is in chapter 6, where we read about the conspiracy of the presidents and governors against this outsider, and doubt his influence with King Darius—who had ascended to the throne because of the victory of the Medes and Persians over the Babylonians.

The penalty for prayer had already been announced, but the Scripture says:

> When Daniel knew that the document was signed, he entered his house (now in his roof chamber he had windows open toward Jerusalem); and he continued kneeling on his knees three times a day, praying and giving thanks before his God, as he had been doing previously. Then these men came by agreement and found Daniel making petition and supplication before his God" (Daniel 6:10-11 NASB).

The hearty conviction of youth had not dimmed with maturity. Daniel was an old man, and he had known political intrigue in one of the greatest pagan capitals the world has ever seen. He was serving in the administration of a third monarch and apparently was still very highly esteemed for his skill and integrity. He did not ostentatiously display his spiritual life or deliberately flaunt a religion which he considered superior to that of the Babylonians. He did not pray in the marketplace or in the palace, but rather in the quiet of his own room. Only by invading his privacy could his enemies find fault with his behavior.

How much better we might be as leaders if we would pray more and talk less–if we would pray more and *worry* less! But let our praying be of Daniel's kind–a personal and private relationship between the leader and his God.

Willingness to Intercede

Another great prayer of the prophet is found in chapter 9, which also contains the important vision of the "seventy weeks." This is a model prayer of leadership because it demonstrates concern not only for the leader himself, but even more so for the people for whom he is responsible. Daniel confessed not his *own* sin, but the sin of the people. As Culver puts it:

> The model "pray-er" associates himself completely with his people. How easy it might have been for Daniel, since he really had lived an exemplary life, to disassociate himself in thought, sympathy, affection, and confession from his people. But this is not the force of his words.
>
> The pastor or missionary (or Sunday School teacher) who would help his people must be one of them in life, thought, affection, and interest. Does not Daniel make us think of Him who though being in the form of God, thought it not a thing to be grasped to be equal with God but took upon Himself the form of a servant and was made in the likeness of men (cf. Phil. 2:6-7)?

There are few models of leadership in the entire Scripture as fruitful for our study as Daniel. The responsibility which he held, the blessings of God which were poured out upon him, and the practical demonstration of his life make this book a focal point of Scripture for all leaders. Let us not forget the central motive of everything Daniel did–faithfulness toward God and consistency toward men. Daniel was a fellow who could be counted on. He was dependable, responsible, and full of genuine integrity. May his kind increase in our day.

Ezra: The Leader as Teacher

12

Ezra was neither a king nor a prophet. A descendant of the line of Aaron through Zadok and Phinehas, he grew up in an alien land (see Ezra 7:1-5). But the priesthood meant very little in Babylon, miles away from the Holy Land and the temple site. The Israelites had been in captivity for 50 years or more, but new hope arose after the entrance into Babylon of Cyrus the Great in 539 B.C.

The first return to the land was led by Zerubbabel (or Sheshbazzar, as some think his Persian name was) in 520 B.C. The second was led by Ezra in 457 B.C. and the third by Nehemiah in 445 B.C. Thus, many Jews were back in the land years before Ezra led the second phase of return.

Ezra's task was distinctly spiritual and pedagogical. Religious conditions among the returned exiles were inadequate, and Ezra appealed to the king of Persia that he be allowed to return as a scribe to his people (see Ezra 7:6).

It is impossible to accurately understand the role of Ezra until we know what a scribe was in his day. A definition which appears in the *Zondervan Pictorial Bible Dictionary* is brief and to the point: one of "a class of learned men who made the systematic study of law and its exposition their professional occupation."[1]

Ezra was not concerned with the politics of the emerging state; nor was he a military leader of any dimension. He was a teacher, and it was to bridge the gap between law and life that he returned to Jerusalem.

Sometimes there is confusion between Ezra and Nehemiah, inasmuch as the story of Ezra does not begin until the seventh chapter of the book which bears his name. Yet, that story continues through most of the Book of Nehemiah. Actually, the men were contemporaries. Nehemiah 8:9 states their relationship quite clearly–Nehemiah was the governor; Ezra, the priest and scribe.

Verse 10 of Ezra 7 is a complimentary commentary on the character of this man. The Scripture records that: "Ezra had prepared his heart to seek the law of the Lord, and to do it, and to teach in Israel statutes and judgments." This is certainly a fitting guideline for any age.

Teaching an Unwilling Congregation in an Alien Culture

The people who had returned to the land were hardly a model "church." They had intermarried, adopted pagan customs, and virtually obliterated the distinction between the Jews returning from Babylon and the half-breed Samaritans inhabiting the land in their absence (see Ezra 9:1-4).

Although there was a favorable response to Ezra's teaching ministry, we should not conclude that the people were eagerly awaiting to hear his cry for a return to holiness. There were other things to do than think about the purity of the law–and, no doubt, Ezra found his constituency in desperate need of revival. Indeed, even after Ezra had ministered for 12 years, we find Nehemiah fasting and praying because the situation in the land was still deplorable (see Neh. 1:4).

But Ezra provides a model for us; he tackled the task with vigor and enthusiasm. He did not tell God it could not be done; nor did he complain about its difficulty. His own spiritual life influenced the development of the people to whom he ministered. Although at times Ezra did not appear thoroughly open-minded, he certainly was open-hearted and genuinely sought to minister in God's way.

It was difficult enough to face the battle of deteriorating spiritual life among his *own* people, but Ezra was also confronted with Samaritan plots to thwart any efforts to unify and develop the returned exiles. Long before he arrived on the scene, the "people of the land" had attempted to halt the rebuilding of the temple and had carried on a general harassment of Zerubbabel and his programs (see Ezra 4:1-5). This continuing struggle was passed on from Zerubbabel to Ezra and Nehemiah. There was no shortage of troublemakers in Israel during those days. If God's leaders did not have to grapple with Bishlam, Rehum, or Shimshai (see Ezra 4:7-8), it would be Sanballat, Tobiah, or Geshem the Arabian (see Neh. 6:1).

Yet, that has always been the lot of God's remnant people. The environment has never been a comfortable or congenial one, whether Egypt or Rome decided its cultural flavor. Today, too, we teach in an alien culture. No Christian leader whose primary responsibility is teaching can forget for a minute that he is proclaiming a countercultural truth system. His ethics and morals fly in the face of much contemporary opinion. Insofar as he is able to stand against this opposition and press the point of scriptural truth, he is following in the pattern of Ezra the scribe.

Teaching the Difficult Subjects

There were a number of controversial issues facing Ezra and Nehemiah–such as the matters of the building of the wall, the abolition of usury, and the clarification of exactly who was welcome to participate in the development of the land. But surely nothing plagued the spiritual life of the people as much as their constant relationship with the half-pagan natives of Canaan.

In that general category, the one specific issue of confusion and difficulty was the matter of divorce and remarriage. When one reads the tenth chapter of Ezra, he is tempted to think that things haven't changed much over the many hundreds of years separating Ezra's day from ours.

Opinions differ on what Ezra should have done about this problem. Certainly the general principle of separation from pagan surroundings is a biblical one in any age and place. But whether the men of Israel should have put away the pagan wives whom they married upon their return to the land is a matter of question. Some would definitely argue that this was the only way to complete a fully biblical separation and to root out sin from the congregation. And the people do seem to have complied quite willingly with Ezra's suggestion.

William Sanford LaSor suggests that Ezra's decision was questionable:

> There is no question that there was real danger in the situation. But here were families that had been established for years, and Ezra insisted that all of the men divorce their wives. Of course, not all of them went along with it; many of them refused. But this was a questionable decision on Ezra's part. We never hear any more of him after that; he seems to have lost his prestige and his authority with the people for good. Nehemiah seems to have modified the rule to prevent future mixed marriages without dissolving the existing ones.[2]

The faithful teacher of God's Word will find himself facing controversial issues many times during his ministry. Indeed, the more alien the culture in which he ministers, the more numerous will be the issues on which he is challenged. I do not know whether Ezra's decision was a good one or not. I do know that he had the courage to face a controversial problem and deal with it. Nothing is ever gained in the spiritual development of God's people if we, their teachers, duck out of important issues just because they are controversial.

However, that is not to say that a rabid dogmatism which advances only one position on a questionable issue is the best plan of attack. I rather take the position that dogmatism, except in the very essentials of Christian faith, is an unattractive posture for a teacher.

One thing is sure—the more difficult and controversial the subject we teach, the more we will have to depend upon the guidance of the Spirit of God. Thus, the more study we will have to do—so that we clearly understand the question, its various alternatives, and the consequences of those alternatives.

Teaching through the Written Word

Sometimes we take the Bible for granted. We have so many copies of it in various versions that we do not think of how it came into existence. Actually, the Old Testament, written under the inspiration of God, was put down in the original manuscript in varying forms and languages. David's scribes would have used a different approach than would Moses or Joshua.

There seems to be good evidence that Ezra and the men of the great synagogue were responsible for collecting and restoring the Scriptures as a complete entity during the construction of the second temple. They also standardized them editorially. Merrill F. Unger writes:

> What was true of the people at large was eminently true of the spiritual leaders. From the time of Ezra, and doubtless long before, there was a special guild of *sopherim*, or scribes, whose special business was to copy the sacred text and meticulously reproduce and hand down the correct reading. In the light of these strict measures, which were taken to insure that every fresh copy was an exact reproduction of the original, it is arbitrary and nonsensical to maintain that each new manuscript was "a new edition." Only the exigencies of the critical theory can obscure the fact that such measures had been taken, not only from the time

> of Ezra, but (and there is no reason to suppose the contrary) continuously from the times of Moses and Joshua on down. The nation which was providentially chosen to be the recipient and custodian of the Sacred Oracles was also providentially endowed with a veneration and concern for the text to insure its correct transmission.[3]

So Ezra, like Paul, had a veneration for books—and particularly for the Book of books. He saw teaching not only as a verbal explanation of the written Word of God, but also as a constant awareness of the importance of that written Word and its transmission to future generations.

Let this be a clarion call to Sunday school teachers, pastors, and Christian leaders in our day. Since God chose to give His Word in written form, it is our task to teach our students to honor that form and to be concerned with its perpetuation, as well as its explanation.

There is a practical side to this last lesson from Ezra's example. Sunday school students will never develop a reverence for revelation and a seriousness in study until they see that pattern in their teachers. There must also be a constant use of the Bible in the classroom. Unlike some religious groups which emphasize the handling of holy writings only by some special leaders, evangelical Christianity proclaims the necessity of all believers being Bible students.

In Ezra we find the beautiful model of what it means for the leader to be a teacher.

John the Baptist: Courage and Clarity

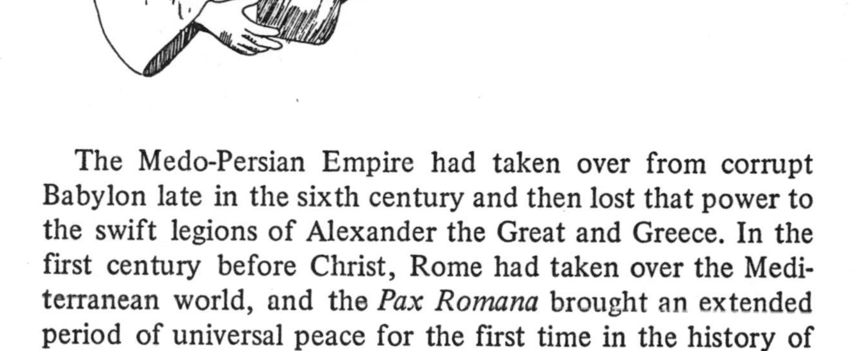

The Medo-Persian Empire had taken over from corrupt Babylon late in the sixth century and then lost that power to the swift legions of Alexander the Great and Greece. In the first century before Christ, Rome had taken over the Mediterranean world, and the *Pax Romana* brought an extended period of universal peace for the first time in the history of the civilized world.

Into this world which He had prepared culturally, politically, and religiously, the Heavenly Father sent His own incarnate Self in the form of His Son. But before the actual appearance of the Messiah, there was to be a demonstration of Old Testament prophecy once again. Four hundred silent years had elapsed. The clarion call which the nation of Israel had not heard since the days of the Captivity would echo again up and down the sunbaked plains of Judaea and particularly by the Jordan River.

John the Baptist remains the unique link between the Old and New Testaments. Since he died before the crucifixion and resurrection of Jesus, he was certainly a part of the pre-Christian era. But as the announcer of the Messiah's presence, he stands with a foot in the New Testament world.

Bursting upon the scene of human history, John the Baptist presents us, also, with a model of leadership which offers unique lessons. The lessons to be learned from John are just as necessary, just as up to date in the decade of the 1980s, as they were at a time when the world was about to slip quietly from "B.C." to "A.D."

Chosen by God

The text in the first chapter of Luke says it well, though in a subtle fashion. He wrote, "His name is John" (Luke 1:63). The Scriptures tell us: "The neighbors were all filled with awe, and throughout the hill country of Judea people were talking about all these things. Everyone who heard this wondered about it, asking, 'What then is this child going to be?' For the Lord's hand was with him" (Luke 1:65-66 NIV).

In this characteristic of leadership, John the Baptist was no different than Joshua or any other leader from Moses to the present hour. Christian leadership is not to be sought in the sense that it is grasped or usurped by the servant. It is rather thrust upon one in God's time and by God's hand. Oh, to be sure, it can be grasped—and probably frequently is. But at that very point it is no longer "Christian leadership" in the best biblical sense, for the very dimension of choosing can't be overlooked if the scriptural pattern is to be followed.

Of course, one can volunteer for various kinds of ministry, but there is a world of difference between volunteering and usurping a position—particularly when that position puts one in authority. Many are the headaches and heartaches of the leader; and James was wise to suggest that believers should not too readily lay hands upon positions of responsibility.

But when God calls, that is a different thing. Then come also the promise of the empowering of His Spirit and the guarantee of blessing, though that blessing may be measured in God's time rather than man's. John the Baptist was hardly a success when judged by human standards, but in the book of heaven he will always be recorded as one who was chosen by God.

Culturally Unusual

It might even be an understatement to say that John the Baptist was culturally unusual! The comparison need not be with our sophisticated modern age, although one might imagine John more at home in some contemporary commune than in the streets of Jerusalem, even in his own time. The population went out to see the unique and striking figure of a man whose clothes were made of camel's hair and were fastened around the waist with a leather belt. As if that were not enough, he lived on locust and wild honey and probably looked very much like a youthful recluse (he was only slightly over 30 years old at the time).

Some months or even years later, when John was in prison, Jesus gave His own testimony to this cultural phenomenon:

> What did you go out into the desert to see? A reed swayed by the wind? If not, what did you go out to see? A man dressed in fine clothes? No, those who wear fine clothes are in kings' palaces. Then what did you go out to see? A prophet? Yes, I tell you, and more than a prophet. This is the one about whom it is written: "I will send my messenger ahead of you, who will prepare your way before you." I tell you the truth: Among those born of women there has not risen anyone greater than John the Baptist. . ." (Matt. 11:7-11 NIV).

To be sure, dressing and eating differently do not make a leader. But on the other hand, the genuinely alert Christian has always been a countercultural phenomenon. That is, he is always out of touch with the world to some measure because he marches to the beat of a different drummer. Paul talks about being a citizen of a heavenly kingdom, and the writer of the Book of Hebrews calls believers "strangers and pilgrims" (see Heb. 11:13). John would certainly qualify for either of those designations and, as such, he sets a model for us today.

In what way are we culturally unusual? To be sure, some Christians want to designate their difference from the world by dress or other kinds of observable habits. They should not be criticized for that choice, because it is the choice that John the Baptist made as well. But more important than the difference in John's appearance was the difference in his attitude. His receptivity of the Messiah, his example of repentance, and his commitment to the task God had given him were what really marked him apart from other men of his day.

Courageous in the Face of Opposition

It did not take long for the curious Pharisees and Sadducees to head out to the Jordan to see this unusual character who was drawing away their congregations. Nor did it take John the Baptist very long to decide what God's message was to them.

> But when he saw many of the Pharisees and Sadducees come to his baptism, he said unto them, O generation of vipers, who hath warned you to flee from the wrath to come? Bring forth therefore fruits meet for repentance: and think not to say within yourselves, We have Abraham to our father: for I say unto you, that God is able of these stones to raise up children unto Abraham. And now also the axe is laid unto the root of the trees: therefore every tree which bringeth not forth good fruit is hewn down, and cast into the fire (Matt. 3:7-10).

It is probably quite characteristic that John's primary opposition came not from paganism, but from the organized religionists. That is not to say that the Christian leader today finds himself opposing the organized church—for in our day such opposition is normally not necessary. Nevertheless, the greatest opposition to Moses came from his own people, the very ones he delivered from Egypt. Daniel was opposed by his own son, and Jesus was detrayed by His own disciple. It is wise, in the light of these lessons, for the Christian leader to expect opposition from those who really ought to be supporting his cause.

When that opposition comes, God surely expects us to maintain a posture of courage. He urged Joshua to this kind of courage in the first chapter of the book which bears his name. It is reflected again and again in all the great leaders of the Bible and is certainly depicted in the behavior of John the Baptist.

Clear in Purpose and Message

What a refreshing wind on the desert! What a delightful breeze after so many barren years without a clearcut message! The fact that John was baptizing was hardly a change from what religious groups had been doing many years before he came on the scene. But the demonstration of purpose and clarity in his message was a new thing on the horizon. He boldly stated that his baptism had only the value of a demonstration of repentance. But the One Who was to follow was much more powerful than the forerunner and ". . . he shall baptize you with the Holy Ghost, and with fire" (Matt. 3:11).

In the first chapter of the Gospel of John, the Baptist identified his own purpose: "I am the voice of one crying in the wilderness, make straight the way of the Lord" (John 1:23). There was never any obscurity in his mind as to what God had called him to do, although a moment of doubt did come upon him when he was thrown into prison a bit later. When the Messiah came, he did not hesitate a moment to say: "Behold the Lamb of God, which taketh away the sin of the world. This is he of whom I said, after me cometh a man which is preferred before me: for he was before me" (John 1:29-30).

How the world needs to hear a clear message with a clear purpose in our day! Sunday school teachers and pastors must stand before their classes and congregations with a firm word from the Lord, but also a demonstration that the authority is God's alone and not resident in the leader himself.

Committed to Christ

One of the most beautiful lessons from the leadership of John the Baptist is found in the latter part of the third chapter of the Gospel of John. John's disciples were, quite naturally, jealous of his popularity and ministry. As soon as it became apparent that the popularity of Jesus would surpass that of John, they reported this very unfortunate happening to their leader.

> John answered and said, a man can receive nothing, except it be given him from heaven. Ye yourselves bear me witness, that I said, I am not the Christ, but that I am sent before him. He that hath the bride is the bridegroom: but the friend of the bridegroom, which standeth and heareth him, rejoiceth greatly because of the bridegroom's voice: this my joy therefore is fulfilled. He must increase, but I must decrease (John 3:27-30).

In my opinion, there is no more beautiful moment in the life and ministry of John the Baptist. Far to be preferred even over the thundering prophet by the river is this meek and gracious man who stepped back into the shadows so that Jesus could have all the glory—and indeed, all of the followers.

What a contrast with the Adult Department Sunday school teacher who fights the superintendent when the question comes up as to whether some of the members of that class can leave the class to become teachers in other divisions of the Sunday school! What a contrast to the clamor in business meetings over who gets what percentage of the budget!

Only complete commitment to Jesus Christ can produce genuinely biblical leadership. Only when we advance His cause, even though it might be to the detriment of our own, can we expect His blessing and the kind of joy in leadership that He wants us to have.

Jesus: How to Work with a Small Group

14

There is no question in the pages of the New Testament but that the primary purpose of the coming of Jesus was to die for the sins of man. In the great act of the incarnation, God became man so that man might live forever with God. Any reference to Jesus as a misguided martyr or as One whose primary role was that of Teacher is a distortion of the central theme of the Gospel—which is the cross of Calvary.

Nevertheless, even though teaching was only an auxiliary goal of our Lord's earthly ministry, He demonstrated the greatest example of teaching the world has ever seen. Not only that, but He exhibited the process of group dynamics (with 12 men) which can stand to the present hour as a model for group activity.

The Leader Must Know His Group

Each of the 12 apostles—even Judas—was of special importance in the group ministry of our Lord. To be sure, they are frequently referred to in group designation—as "the disciples" or "the Twelve." But when it came down to the specific ministry which the Lord had for them, it is apparent that He knew each one in a very special way.

With Peter, Jesus tended to be blunt, even harsh at times, so that the rough fisherman would understand the point. With John, He was always tender, apparently because He knew John's gentle disposition. With Thomas, the skeptic, He was patient. Different men with different personalities and different needs drew from our Lord different responses in leadership and group behavior.

Quite obviously the same principle applies in our day to pastors, Sunday school teachers, and other church workers. It is impossible for us to follow the example of our Lord in building and equipping disciples unless we see how much of an effort He put forth to understand persons as individuals. We might say of our Lord and His disciples that He:

1. Selected them carefully;
2. Handled them individually;
3. Taught them faithfully.

One incident during the earthly ministry of our Lord recorded in John chapter 6, pinpoints this special understanding He had for His disciples. After the feeding of the 5,000 and the sermon on the Bread of Life, many of His nominal followers left Him because they misunderstood His spiritual application regarding the eating of His flesh and the drinking of His blood. As the multitudes moved away from that invitation, Jesus turned to the Twelve and asked, "Will ye also go away?" (v. 67).

The response of Peter was prophetic, whereupon Jesus reminded them that He had chosen each one of them and yet one was "a devil" (John 6:70). Yet, even to this one the Lord extended the privilege of meeting with the disciples until the final hour in the upper room and, some believe, offered him the opportunity to repent even before the deed was finally carried out.

How well do you know the group God has given you to

work with? Do you *really* know them? Have you visited in their homes? Do you know their hurts and heartaches? Are you able to pray for them with specific requests? Are you trusting God for wisdom to work with them as individuals, applying different techniques to different needs?

The Leader Must Teach His Group

Group leadership in the church is the long-term process of building one's life into others. Paul capsulized it in brief, but potent, form when he wrote to Timothy: "The things that thou hast heard of me among many witnesses, the same commit thou to faithful men, who shall be able to teach others also" (2 Tim. 2:2).

Jesus taught the disciples continually during His entire three and one-half year ministry, but a highlight of that teaching was in His explanation of the parabolic method recorded in Matthew 13. Jesus indicated that the parables blinded and confused the Pharisees, but at the same time caused learning and growth on the part of the disciples. To the disciples, it was given "to know the mysteries of the kingdom of heaven," but not so those whose hearts were hardened with unbelief (v. 11). The disciples were privileged above all who had gone before to hear from the mouth of the blessed Lord Himself an exposition of the meaning of the Old Testament.

> But blessed are your eyes, for they see: and your ears, for they hear. For verily I say unto you, that many prophets and righteous men have desired to see those things which ye see, and have not seen them; and to hear those things which ye hear, and have not heard them" (Matt. 13:16-17).

Here again, the example is plain for us. Every Christian is charged with discipling responsibilities. He may be discipling only one or two people whom he has led to Christ, or those lives God is allowing him to influence in an important way. He may find his discipling ministries primarily in his own family with children that God has placed there under his care and protection. Of course, the Sunday school teacher is a discipler. So, too, are the children's church leader, the youth director, and the pastor. In the Great Commission, Jesus told us that making disciples involves teaching (see Matt. 28:19-20). It is not just the informal impact of life upon life—as important as that *is*. It is a deliberate and sustained effort to communicate God's truth to others.

So every group leader is a group teacher. The more thorough and efficient his teaching becomes, the more he reflects the example of the Lord Jesus in working with a small group. Whatever else the disciples were, they were learners; and it is clear that Jesus had some very specific goals for their educational pattern.

The Leader Must Be Patient with His Group

Patience seems to have been as much a part of the character of our Lord as it is unlike many of us. On numerous occasions during the years of their time together, Jesus found it necessary to exercise the greatest patience with these slow learners who somehow didn't even understand the whole process when they saw the empty tomb and the risen Lord. Of course, we must not be too hard on the disciples, because theirs was a unique experience not to be compared to anything before or since. Our focus is not upon the need for patience in their leader, but rather upon the Lord's willingness to provide it.

In John chapter 11, we have the record of the raising of Lazarus. A most interesting conversation preceded the actual miracle, when Jesus used the euphemism "sleep" for death in saying: "Our friend Lazarus sleepeth; but I go, that I may awake him out of sleep" (v. 11). The disciples were glad that Lazarus was resting comfortably and indicated a favorable prognosis. The Lord had to respond very bluntly by saying, "Lazarus is dead" (v. 14). Then He added the interesting statement of verse 15: "And I am glad for your sakes that I was not there, to the intent ye may believe; nevertheless let us go unto him."

Even at the moment of the death of His friend, Jesus' primary concern was for the learning of the disciples. He knew what He was about to do and that Lazarus was in no danger, but He wanted them to see a miracle of resurrection rather than a miracle of healing.

How often at times like this the Lord must have been tempted to scold His group and chide them for not knowing more accurately the things they ought to have known. Sometimes they defied Him openly, as did Peter and Thomas on two separate occasions. Sometimes they just reflected a simple ignorance of many of the things He had been trying to explain to them. Yet in spite of it all, the Lord just kept repeating and responding in love and patience.

Through it all, the disciples constantly tried to grasp the nature and character of their leader. Their frequent lapses into unbelief and failure to understand the Lord are graphic demonstrations of the reality of the Bible account of how the Lord worked with His group. Stephen Neill writes:

> One of the reasons for accepting as reliable the picture of the disciples presented to us in the Gospels is that it is so entirely free of idealization, and is, in fact, unflattering rather than the reverse. It is psychologically apt, as an account of the attempt of a group of average men to understand a Leader whose gifts were so transcendently greater than their own.[1]

Our hang-up with this point is to argue that Jesus could summon the necessary patience because He was God; but we, like the members of our groups, are finite human beings, subject to the same failings and faults as they are. But this is precisely where the Holy Spirit enters the picture. He can change personalities, and can create in the life of the group leader a spirit of patience and long-suffering to enable him to carry out his task—even in the face of ignorance or rebellion.

The Leader Must Spend Time with His Group

In his most helpful book, *The Training of the Twelve* (Harper), A. B. Bruce suggests that the Gospels taken together report only 33 or 34 actual days of activity in the total ministry of our Lord. He then raises the question as to what the Lord did with the rest of the time. The title of his book is a giveaway as to what Bruce thinks about the answer–Jesus spent most of His time with His disciples, teaching and training them.

The Lord's ministry was not primarily to the multitudes, although we see some magnificent demonstrations of His public oratory. His real teaching effort was spent on His disciples, with whom He maintained constant contact and upon whose lives He exercised constant influence. But such influence is not sustained by an occasional class meeting. The Lord literally lived with these 12 men for weeks on end. William Sanford LaSor writes a beautiful paragraph describing this continuous relationship:

> They saw Him under all conditions: when He was hungry, passing through a field of grain; when He was tired, stretched out in the boat. They saw Him when religious officialdom prodded Him with sticky questions; they saw Him when a sinful woman washed His feet with tears of devotion because her sins had been forgiven. They saw Him bless little children; they saw Him drive moneychangers out of the temple. They saw Him under every possible condition that could occur for about a year or more. Then one day Jesus said to them, "Whom say ye that I am?" Peter spoke up, "Thou art the Christ, the Son of the living God" (Matt. 16:15-16). No man who has lived with me for a year is going to say anything like that about me–and I don't believe they will say it about you. But they said it about Jesus.[2]

Each of us has a group of some kind–and therefore a responsibility to respond to that group according to the example that Jesus set. The type of group makes no difference, for the principles demonstrated by the Lord Jesus are universal in application and timeless in value.

Peter: A Personal Invitation to Leadership

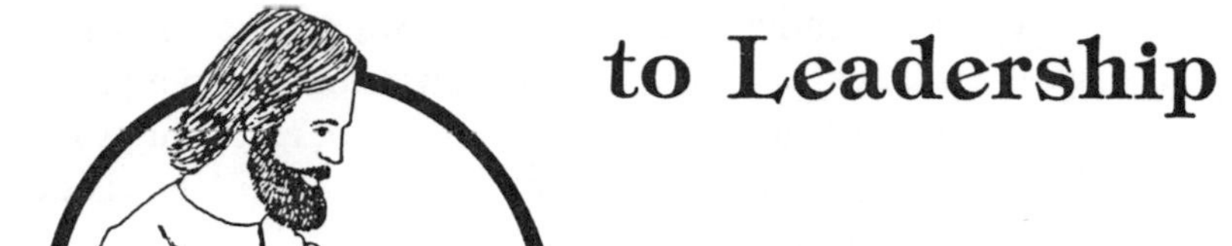

15

As we noted in the last chapter, the ministry of Jesus was not primarily to large groups of people. True, there were those great events when thousands of people gathered to hear Him preach or watch His miracles, but essentially the central thrust of His ministry was to twelve men. Within that band of twelve, there were three to whom He seemed to give quite personal attention—Peter, James, and John—and of those three, it would appear from reading the text of the New Testament, that Peter received more special handling than any of the other disciples.

This point comes out most clearly in John 21. The chapter opens with Peter and six other disciples on a fishing expedition. It is difficult to say whether they were going out fishing just for the night or whether Peter was really returning to his former occupation.

We must remember that although the resurrection had occurred and the disciples had seen the risen Lord, at this point they did not know where He was, nor did they have any idea what their next step should be. In the confusion and frustration of that moment, Peter turned back to the one thing he knew and loved best in all of life—fishing.

Was Peter questioning his own call to leadership on this occasion? I do not know. Certainly, however, the lesson of the passage is clear. Once Christ has put His hand upon a person for a distinctive form of Christian leadership, returning to his former occupation, no matter how noble it might be, is out of the will of God for that person.

Such an exchange is not uncommon in our lives today. In fact, in the rushing, sophisticated society in which we live, there are so many more things to attract our attention away from the will of God for our lives. Satan makes sure there are many distractions, many very valuable and good things to which we can turn our attention and our time, when Christ is all the time waiting for us to give complete commitment to the task He has assigned to us.

Most Christian leaders, at one time or another during their years of ministry, have questioned the call of God and His hand upon their lives. In these moments of weakness it is even more important to recognize that the Lord is on the shore waiting to deal with us personally if need be.

A Private Lesson

The last half of the final chapter in the Gospel of John is one of my favorite portions of Scripture. To think that God in human flesh would spend time with one recalcitrant disciple to help him overcome his stubbornness and shortcomings so that he might be the kind of leader the Early Church would desperately need is a striking revelation.

It all happened after breakfast, according to John 21:15, and the conversation began around the central theme of motivation for Christian leadership. Peter was not scolded for his fishing trip, nor did the Lord question for a moment his behavior of the preceding days. The key issue was the matter of love—"Simon, son of Jonas, lovest thou me?" The central motive of Christian service is love for Jesus Christ. Love for others may come along in a secondary role and, indeed, is a New Testament concept. But foundational to love for others is love for Christ, and it is that question which Christ was asking Peter on this occasion.

How closely we can relate this conversation to preceding events, such as Peter's denial, is certainly open to question. Also open to question is whether the different words for "love" used in the passage really convey different meanings. I rather think they do, but not all New Testament scholars take that position.

As the passage moves on, it becomes apparent that the Lord wanted Peter to understand *Christian leadership as a rejection of selective obedience in favor of an acceptance of complete commitment.* He would no longer be able to decide his own fate, but he was now a disciple whose allegiance to his Lord in all things was to be unimpeachable. Not only that, but Christ would not allow His leader to look at others for a comparison of God's dealing with him. John 21:21-22 is a pungent demand for single-mindedness.

Speaking in the contemporary idiom, we would say that Jesus' response to Peter meant, in effect: "Whatever I do with other people is none of your business. If you are to be a disciple, a Christian leader of the first rank, your obedience is to be to me without any concern on your part for how I deal with others."

What a lesson that is for us today! How easy it is for us to take our eyes off Jesus and look instead at others whose positions in the body of Christ may seem less burdensome or more rewarding. But the Lord of the Church will have none of such behavior, and He demands complete commitment of ourselves to Him.

Accepting Responsibility

The leadership of Peter in the Early Church emerged even before the coming of the Holy Spirit. In the first chapter of the Book of Acts, he appears as the one who "stood up in the midst of the disciples" (v. 15). Peter and the other disciples seemed to understand the former's unique role of leadership. Of course, evangelical Christians do not equate this with any form of apostolic succession. Somebody had to be the leader; and in the plan of Christ, Peter was selected.

The scene in our passage is located in Jerusalem at the end of a 40-day period which Jesus spent with His disciples after the resurrection. At Bethany, probably on the southeastern side of the Mount of Olives, the ascension took place in full view of the gathered disciples. After returning to Jerusalem, Peter asserted his leadership immediately—with the suggestion that a successor to Judas should be chosen. Please note that he merely presided at the meeting. He did not select Matthias or even nominate him.

Many commentators have criticized Peter for this particular action and indicated that the "open slot" in the disciple band of 12 was to have been reserved for the Apostle Paul. But that is pure speculation and does not rest on any solid biblical foundation. As a matter of fact, the text of Scripture never criticizes Peter or the other disciples for this little election session, and we have every reason to believe that the Lord answered their prayer of Acts 1:24 in the manner to which these Jewish brethren were accustomed—the casting of lots.

I have indicated in the heading of this section the central lesson which I think we must learn from it—Peter's willingness to accept responsibility. We continue to have problems in the evangelical Church of our day with this matter. True, we generally do not have enough willing workers at all levels, but it becomes increasingly more difficult to recruit when the ideas of "leadership" and "responsibility" shade the task under question. For example, there are people who are willing to help in the Sunday school class, but who will not take the teaching responsibility. Or there are folks who are willing to serve on the committee, but who will not chair. Sometimes I wonder whether the opposite of responsibility isn't really irresponsibility, although we usually do not speak that negatively regarding those who seem unwilling to accept a task.

Certainly, there is the element of fear involved here as well as the hesitancy to undertake something for which one is not thoroughly prepared. But that could have been Peter's excuse, too. He took the responsibility at Jerusalem in Acts 1 because he felt called of God to do so, not because he had graduated from the best seminary or was eminently qualified to lead the business meeting and begin to head up the work of the Church. Certainly, the central factor in the establishment of church leadership is twofold: a gifting by the Holy Spirit and then a calling by the Lord of the Church. Both of these, held in proper balance, will deliver us from laziness on the one hand, and from pride on the other.

Public Ministry

Once Peter's public ministry began on the Day of Pentecost, it did not end until his death. Public ministry for Peter was inseparably linked with preaching; so at the instigation of the Holy Spirit, he began immediately—as the record indicates in Acts 2:14. It is no doubt important to understand that Peter once again stood up "with the eleven." He may have been the star of the show, so to speak, but he was not a soloist. The work of the Early Church was always a team effort, and Peter's role was to be a team leader and spokesman. His first sermon of the Early Church was dynamite, and William Sanford LaSor indicates the direction it took:

> Peter's sermon applied the sword to the consciences of his hearers. If Jesus was indeed God's anointed, and they had been responsible for His crucifixion, what should they do? Peter replied in clear terms, "Repent, and be baptized every one of you in the name of Jesus Christ for the remission of sins, and ye shall receive the gift of the Holy Ghost. For the promise is unto you, and to your children, and to all that are afar off, even as many as the Lord our God shall call" (Acts 2:38-39). This is not all that Peter

> said—he used "many other words"—but this is quite sufficient. It opens the door wide for all who repent to come back to God through Jesus Christ. Some say that Peter and Paul, in their theology, are poles apart. Cullmann not only rejects this notion, but says, "Indeed, I should go even further and definitely assert that within the circle of the Twelve, he (Peter) is the one who in this respect *stands closest to Paul*."[1]

So, the lessons in the life of Peter are demonstrably relevant for our world today. When God calls, we must answer—not only with a response of willingness, but also with a genuine commitment to the assuming of responsibility. Someone once said, "The greatest ability is responsibility." May God give us in our churches today Sunday school teachers, superintendents, youth leaders, pastors, and many other types of church workers who are willing to recognize God's personal invitation to them through Christ to positions of leadership.

Stephen: A Layman Makes His Mark

Division between the laity and clergy was not at all pronounced in the New Testament. Today, a person who has formal training for ministry is hired by a congregation to serve as its pastor, and he makes his living in the ministry. He is clearly identified as a "minister" or, to be technical, a "clergyman." But whatever posture one assumes in church polity, it must be said that such a distinction was not specifically made in the days of the Early Church.

I have called Stephen a layman because in our modern sense he would be just that. He was one of the band of believers in the Early Church who was selected by his peers to care for the daily distribution to the poor. The event which gave rise to such an appointment was the complaint of the Greek-speaking Jews that their widows were not being properly dealt with in the daily distribution.

Though Stephen's ministry, short as it was, was filled with far more than just the task to which he was appointed, it seems quite safe to say that he was basically a layman in the carrying out of his tasks. Inasmuch as that is true, he provides us with a beautiful lesson of lay leadership.

We have seen a much stronger concept of lay involvement emerging in this decade of the 1970s. Perhaps Christ is forcing His Church back again to a much more biblical view of the makeup of His Body, in which the distinctions between clergy and laity are not as pronounced as history has drawn them. Whatever the reasons, whatever the motivations, Stephen was "a man for all seasons" and specifically, a man for our season today.

Spiritual Qualities

"Wherefore, brethren, look yet out among you seven men of honest report, full of the Holy Ghost and wisdom, whom we may appoint over this business. . . . And Stephen, full of faith and power, did great wonders and miracles among the people" (Acts 6:3, 8).

The context tells us that the twelve apostles summoned the members of the Early Church and requested that they search among their own number to find "seven men of honest report, full of the Holy Ghost and wisdom, whom we may appoint over this business" (Acts 6:3). This is clearly a demonstration of organization on the part of the Early Church and, although it might not be referred to specifically as "democracy," it certainly carries that general overview.

Perhaps the best emphasis one could make as a lesson for our leadership techniques in the church of today is the evidence here of what I like to call "participatory leadership." The apostles could very well have selected these men themselves, and no one would have questioned their authority. But in keeping with the Lord's teachings regarding the servant-leader in the church, they passed over to all the people the decision regarding a selection of lay leadership in what we have called the seven deacons.

The qualifications for the office were basically threefold: The men were to be honest, filled with the Spirit, and wise.

We might also indicate that they were to be church members ("out [from] among you"), though not all believers see any identifiable membership roles in the Early Church (Acts 6:3).

The word which appears in Acts 6:3 as the English word "wisdom" is the Greek word *sophia*, which could very well be referred to in this context as common sense or the ability to be very practical in handling the everyday problems of the church. It surely is not to be taken in this context as a reference to philosophical or specialized knowledge of ethereal matters.

In addition to the initial qualities required of all of these seven lay leaders, Stephen demonstrated qualities which are indicated in Acts 6:8: "full of faith and power." Newer translations designate the first of those qualities as "grace," and that would certainly help us understand Stephen's general attitude which is displayed in the seventh chapter. No doubt the innate power was a demonstration of the Spirit-control which his brethren saw in him when they selected him according to the guidelines of verse 3.

What a beautiful designation of spiritual qualities for the selection of lay leadership today! When we look for deacons, trustees, Sunday school teachers, or people who serve Christ through the church in any other capacity, we should still look for people who have a good reputation of honesty and integrity in the congregation; people who are clearly full of the Holy Spirit and controlled by Him; people who are able to apply the wise common sense of mature decision-making and judgment to every situation; and people who are gracious in their behavior to others.

Sometimes we select lay leaders on the assumption that involvement in the ministry of the church will be good for them and may draw them more closely into a relationship with the Lord. But that was never the biblical pattern.

The Apostle Paul gave Timothy clear instructions about the selection of elders and deacons—and those characteristics build upon these primitive ones found in the sixth chapter of the Book of Acts. Stephen was what he was because God had been working in his life before his appointment to leadership. Leadership does not begin on the deacon board or in the Sunday school class, it begins at home in one's personal development of spiritual life and his relationship with his family!

We might also emphasize that Stephen was faithful where he was before he was appointed to a more responsible ministry. It is not possible to talk about his long years of service because his life was snuffed out at the very beginning of his ministry. But he was obedient at whatever level God placed him and, in accordance with biblical patterns. Stephen was regularly awarded more leadership and responsibility.

Emotional Qualities

Acts 6:15 is hardly a demonstration of a list of characteristics, but it does give us a moment of insight into the kind of gracious behavior which characterized this man, Stephen. The New International Version translates the verse this way: "All who were sitting in the Sanhedrin looked intently at Stephen, and they saw that his face was like the face of an angel." Stephen was on trial for heresy because he was accused of speaking blasphemous words against the temple and the law. The text of Scripture indicates, however, that as in the case of Jesus, the arguments against him were trumped up and the charges falsified (Acts 6:10-14). Nevertheless, Stephen was given an opportunity to respond to the charges.

But we are getting just a bit ahead of the story. Our focus at the moment is the attitude and behavior with which Stephen faced the vicious attacks which he knew from the first to be both malicious and slanderous. An account of the passage in a succinct paragraph is offered by C. J. Ellicott:

> We can scarcely be wrong in tracing this description to the impression made at the time on St. Paul, and reported by him to St. Luke. It must be interpreted by the account given of angels as appearing in the form of "young men" (Mark 16:5), and so throw some light upon St. Stephen's age, as being probably about

> the same standing as St. Paul, and implied that his face was lighted up as by the radiance of a divine brightness. . . . Here the impression left by St. Luke's narrative is that the face of St. Stephen was illumined at once with the glow of an ardent zeal and the serenity of a higher wisdom.[1]

Mental Qualities

Sometimes we do not give proper tribute to the importance of mental qualities when selecting Christian leaders. Yet, Stephen's defense, recorded in chapter 7 of the Book of Acts, is a masterpiece of teaching on the part of a layman. It is a brilliant apology, speaking positively regarding the doctrine of the early Christians.

Stephen did not deal with the charges made against him, nor did he mention himself personally. He rather focused upon the central issue of the argument, which many scholars see as the prophetic view of Scripture versus the legalistic view. The mental and intellectual characteristics of this young leader are demonstrable from the beginning of verse 2 right on through the account of his death. He spoke as one who had really done his homework—indeed, as one who had steeped himself in the history of his people, in their traditions, and in the relationship between Old Testament theology and New Testament theology.

Sometimes we, in our day, fail to appreciate the inestimable value of a sanctified intellect. It is always popular to point to Peter and John as ignorant fishermen who were greatly used by God despite their lack of formal training. And that is a truth of history which still happens in our day—praise His name! But what of the others? There were many intellectual giants who saw mental sharpness not as some pitfall of sin and pride but rather as one more gift from God to be returned to Him. Moses, Isaiah, Paul, Luke were just a few of them—men who could serve the cause of heaven better because their God-given intellects had been developed in rigorous training.

No Sunday school teacher should ever be a purveyor of ignorance. But by his own example, as well as by his constant verbal urgings, he should promote the advancement of knowledge toward service for Christ. There are many more opportunities for mentally equipped Christians in today's world than there have ever been before.

To be sure, Stephen was *saved, Spirit-filled,* and *serving.* But he was also *smart*—as his flowing history of Israel in chapter 7 witnesses. He had prepared himself to give back to God a multiplied talent, not a buried one. His speech before the Jewish leaders is a masterpiece of Judeo-Christian doctrine.

It was good Christian doctrine, but it was heresy to the Sanhedrin. Such radical thinking could not be tolerated, and in characteristic dogmatism and unthinking anarchy, they stopped their ears, rushed at him, cast him out of the city, and stoned him. But even in his death, his spiritual, emotional, and mental qualities were maintained, so that hymnwriter Reginald Heber could say of this first Christian martyr:

> The martyr first, whose eagle eye
> Could pierce beyond the grave,
> Who saw his Master in the sky
> And called on Him to save;
> Like Him, with pardon on his tongue,
> In midst of mortal pain,
> He prayed for them that did the wrong.
> Who follows in his train?

James: Serving the Establishment Church

In the early days of the ministry of Jesus, His own half brothers were His most outspoken critics. During the years of His earthly ministry, they seemed second only to the Pharisees and Sadducees in taunting Him with unbelief. The words of our Lord regarding the disrepute of a prophet in his own country did not represent some generalized proverb, but rather directly reflected His own experience.

But something happened after the resurrection. We do not know exactly when or how, but sometime between the resurrection of our Lord and the events following the first missionary journey of Paul, James was converted and became the accepted leader of the Jerusalem church. He is not a dominant figure in New Testament history, but he does emerge in Acts 15 as a solid spokesman for the mother church at Jerusalem.

The events surrounding this particular church meeting really have to do with the issue of legalism. The year was approximately A.D. 50, and the believers had been winning Gentile converts for almost 10 years. But the issue was by no means settled in the church.

The chapter opens by telling us that "certain men which came down from Judaea taught the brethren, and said, Except ye be circumcised after the manner of Moses, ye cannot be saved" (Acts 15:1). This was happening at the church at Antioch, which had been so committed to missionary activity! Note also that it happened immediately upon the excellent report of the missionary journey which Paul had just delivered (see Acts 14:26-28). Satan always knows just when to attack the Church and what issues to use.

The issue of legalism has always been an effective one. Those believers who lean toward a legalistic viewpoint accuse others of license and liberalism. Those who tend more toward a stronger position on liberty criticize people who indicate that certain "don'ts" are necessary for spiritual Christian living.

It may be of value to note that the same issue faced in Acts 15 is the one concerning which the Book of Galatians was written. Someone has said that "Galatianism" is the belief that any action of the flesh can make one more acceptable to God either before or after conversion. In writing the Book of Galatians, Paul referred to this incident in the early verses of chapter 2 and said that the men from Judaea were "false brothers [who] had infiltrated our ranks to spy on the freedom we have in Christ Jesus and to make us slaves" (v. 4 NIV).

Leadership Is Related to the Home Church

Although James is not named in Acts 15 until verse 13, we see the importance of his role in the mother church at Jerusalem. To be sure, Paul and Barnabas did not go to Jerusalem to get "orders from headquarters," but rather to allow an open confrontation and discussion about an issue which threatened to plague the church at all points. This was of critical importance in view of the recent establishment of new congregations in such places as Lystra, Iconium, Pamphylia, Perga, and other towns throughout Asia Minor.

In the group at Jerusalem, there were three dominant leaders–Peter, James, and John. But, although we are accustomed from the Gospels to seeing those three names in concert, we are not talking about James, the brother of John; but James, the half brother of Jesus. Paul said that these three "seemed to be pillars" (Gal. 2:9), which gives definite weight to the leadership role that James must have assumed by this time.

We had every reason to believe that Peter and John would be pillars. After all, they were in the inner band of disciples, they were eyewitnesses to the death and resurrection of Christ, they had looked into the empty tomb, they were present at the coming of the Holy Spirit on the Day of Pentecost, and they possessed every other possible credential for the leadership role. But James was a newcomer. Yet, he is mentioned with equal importance.

Perhaps the single most important lesson here is that James rose to leadership within his own home church. After he came to a position of faith, it was essential for him to establish credibility with the apostles, who knew of his former skepticism. Whether his leadership was advanced because of his close blood relationship to Christ is not known. What we may assume is that he served faithfully and was elevated to leadership by his peers, not because of any external pressure.

Of course, leadership does not begin at the local church, but at home. Nevertheless, we face a situation today with so many para-church organizations doing an excellent work for God that the leadership of the local assembly is sometimes drained off to serve other groups. In one sense, it is correct to say that the local church ought to be thrilled to have this kind of support and willingly give enthusiastically of its people to serve these organizations. On the other hand, it is also biblical to state that such organizations have credence and authenticity only as they serve the Body of Christ and its representation in local churches.

So whatever else James was or was not in the service of Christ, he was a strong churchman. And because of his service and loyalty to the Jerusalem congregation, we find him standing in the place of leadership at a crucial junction in the history of the Early Church.

Leadership Requires a Stand on Convictions

We should note that the opponents of Paul and Barnabas were given every opportunity to speak. Then Peter responded by reminding the gathered assembly of his experience with Cornelius, and concluded that it made no sense to put Gentiles under law which Jewish Christians themselves could not keep. Henry Jacobsen said it well:

> Peter established the fact, then, that Gentiles had been saved without being circumcised or obeying the Ten Commandments. The implication of his remarks was that circumcision and the law, though both were ordained by God, had served their purpose and were no longer necessary.[1]

The glorious conclusion of Peter's remarks is that all people, Jews or Gentiles, are saved through grace on account of their faith—not by any works or law-keeping.

Then James took his turn. It was not his purpose to dominate the meeting or to issue any kind of *ex cathedra* pronouncements. Rather, he wanted to summarize the general opinions of the group. He reiterated Peter's point from the Book of Amos, and he rendered an opinion.

Perhaps the word "sentence" in the Authorized Version is a bit strong (see Acts 15:19). Probably James was chairing the meeting, but he was not a judge passing "sentence" as to what should be done. It rather appears that he was making a suggestion. Salvation, he indicated, should be no more difficult for Gentiles than for Jews, and purely on the basis of the grace of God. Nevertheless, to show some concern for the more conservative element present at the meeting, James diplomatically indicated several guidelines for behavior which should not be viewed as requirements for salvation.

Leadership Involves Participatory Decision-Making

After James' speech, it was still necessary for a decision to be made. He was merely suggesting what should be done, not demanding it. We read in Acts 15:22 that the apostles and elders "with the whole church" decided that the advice was good, that Peter and James had analyzed the situation correctly, and that certain members of the congregation should be sent to Antioch with Paul and Barnabas to carry letters explaining the results of the council.

We are not told exactly how they arrived at that decision. Was there a vote? Was some form of casting lots still used? One thing seems clear—there was a consensus of opinion, and the letters represented the total thinking of the Jerusalem council—not just the decision of James. It is also interesting how properly the council carried out its action by not just sending Paul and Barnabas with the message. After all, these two men had represented one distinct viewpoint in the dispute, and it would hardly have been in good taste to allow them to be the sole carriers of the decision when it distinctly favored their viewpoint. So, the leaders of the Jerusalem church covered their tracks in two ways. They sent written letters explaining exactly what the Antioch church should do regarding Gentile converts, and they sent two of their own people, Judas and Silas, to confirm the content of the letters and, no doubt, assist in the early implementation of the decision.

Though he appears for just a fleeting moment in the pages of the New Testament, James offers us a glimpse of solid leadership. He was faithful in his own church, he was willing to honestly stand by his convictions and yet not force other people to believe what he believed, and he was perfectly content to allow the entire group to have a role in the decision-making process. No wonder Paul referred to him as one of the pillars in the Jerusalem church!

James' example affords us an opportunity to see these qualities at work in a realistic situation. The council at Jerusalem certainly was no "church fight" in the modern sense. Yet, the atmosphere was surely charged with friction and competition. In such surroundings, James emerged as a leader with reason, compassion, and foresight.

These qualities have always been important in the church, but never more so than today. The irrationality of the world system demands that Christian leaders rise to the task of clearheaded and rational responses to the confusion of the surrounding society.

In reality, the church business meeting, such as we see here in Acts 15, is a microcosm of a broader cross section of Christian ministry. Those assembled leaders represent the local church in actual business procedures, but also the universal Church in behavior and demonstration of unity. If we cannot work together in business sessions as a demonstration of unity and love, the world has reason to doubt the validity of our ministry.

So let's be leaders like James—ready for crisis but never precipitating one, and poised for God's use in any situation.

Paul: Leadership Produces Leadership

The Apostle Paul dominates the New Testament much in the way that Moses dominates the Old. In many ways, he stands as the outstanding example of leadership—with the exception of our Lord Himself. And in the sense of leadership being reproductive, there is no person in either the Old or the New Testaments who offers us a greater model of building one's life into others for the cause of Christ than does this complex man from Tarsus.

It is very possible that Paul came from a middle-class family inasmuch as he was born a Roman citizen. The Hebrew name "Saul" means "asked for" and is no doubt connected with Israel's first king from whose tribe (Benjamin) Paul himself also came.

As a boy, Paul was immersed in the curriculum of the synagogue school and studied further during his teen-age years at the feet of the noted scholar, Gamaliel. He was trained to be a rabbi and apparently excelled many of his peers, entering the defense of the Hebrew faith and persecution of Christians with great zeal.

He was most likely always a single man, given throughout all of his adult life to the sacrificial service of the cause that he believed in. Longenecker reminds us, too, that Paul was an urban-centered personality:

> Paul was distinctly a man of the city, with attitudes and experiences which prepared him to think broadly and minister widely. He had been raised in the thriving commercial and intellectual center of Tarsus and trained in the Israelite capital of Jerusalem; he concentrated his missionary activities on the great centers of Roman influence; and he looked forward to preaching in Rome, the capital of the empire. His urbanized outlook is seen in his metaphors, most of which are drawn from city life: the stadium (1 Cor. 9:24-27; Phil. 3:14), the law courts (Rom. 7:1-4; Gal. 3:15; 4:1-2), the processions (2 Cor. 2:14; Col. 2:15), and the market (2 Cor. 1:22; 5:5).[1]

We could select from the life and ministry of Paul many incidents and illustrations to make the point about productive leadership. But one of the most striking passages is his relationship with the Ephesian elders at the end of his ministry. He was, by now, an old and wise leader of the Church. But his early zeal had not abated, nor had he slowed down his activity. He was returning to Jerusalem from the third missionary journey when we find him at Miletus. He did not want to go up to Ephesus–because the time delay might cause him to miss the Feast of Pentecost back at Jerusalem. It is interesting that an independent thinker like Paul should be so concerned about religious traditions.

Servant of the Lord

Ephesus was about 30 miles from Miletus, and the elders of the church went down to visit Paul at his request. There seemed to be an immediate recognition that this was no ordinary meeting. Paul sensed that greater difficulties awaited him in Jerusalem and reminded the elders that they should carry on the work at Ephesus, which he had faithfully taught them to do.

In Acts 20:17-19, Paul refers almost exclusively to himself, indicating the kind of ministry he had at Ephesus. What does a productive leader do with his subordinates? Certainly, one of the answers appears in verse 20: "I kept back nothing that was profitable unto you, but have shewed you, and have taught you publickly, and from house to house."

The productive leader is always a teaching leader. He is always taking time to explain to his subordinates the issues involved—in a way that their own ministries can be made productive by utilizing the things he has learned.

Notice that Paul's remarks here are centered exclusively on his faithful service to Jesus Christ. If the Ephesian elders are to be like their leader, they must learn to serve the Lord with humility of mind, with many tears, and temptations or trials (see Acts 20:19).

Paul was not boasting in these verses, but rather was indicating something of the grace of God which was a part of his life and call. Perhaps that is the key to the success of his leadership. Rather than beginning with a concern for other people, he began with a genuine commitment of servanthood to Christ. It is very apparent, in the pages of the New Testament as well as from our own experience, that we cannot "love the lost" until a definitive love for Christ has been established.

This is not unlike Peter's experience with Christ recorded in the twenty-first chapter of the Gospel of John. The question Jesus asked dealt with Peter's love for Him, rather than his love for other people. To be sure, love for other people is extremely important—and Paul will get to that, but he wants the Ephesian elders to recognize that the proper New Testament perspective of leadership centers in service for Jesus Christ, the Lord.

We have no idea how many men were present on this occasion, or how many churches they represented. Some would indicate that there were several churches in Ephesus and each one sent its "pastor" to this meeting with Paul. Others suggest that surely only one congregation could have been established and that the multiplicity of leaders indicates a plurality of elders in the Early Church. Certainly, neither of those positions can be dogmatically defended. One needs to read the passage carefully and come to his own conclusions.

Another thing that surfaces in these early verses (Acts 20:17-19) is Paul's openness with the Ephesian elders. He reminded them that they knew from the very first day he went into Asia what he was saying and why. He never hid the Gospel, nor did he ever clothe it in obscure terms. He was a vulnerable leader in the fullest sense of that word, and his vulnerability very frequently led him to personal heartache and sorrow.

Servant of the Word

What did Paul teach "publickly, and from house to house" (Acts 20:20)? Verse 24 is a pivotal point indicating his emphasis on the Gospel of the grace of God. Paul's humble "servanthood" led him to a posture of self-denial, even to the point where he could say, "Neither count I my life dear unto myself." The purpose of self-denial was to facilitate goal achievement–namely, carrying out what God wanted Paul to do and the mission which he clearly had in life. Paul was the apostle of the Gentiles. They were to learn from him the message of God's grace that salvation was available to all men everywhere who would put their trust in Jesus.

But Paul did not carry out a ministry of pure evangelism. He had spent three years in Ephesus, during which time he had declared unto the elders there "all the counsel of God" (Acts 20:27). This was edificational ministry in the highest sense. Once people put their trust in Christ and become God's children through His grace, it is no longer necessary to keep proclaiming the Gospel to them. They need to be built up in the things of Christ and to be taught the biblical emphases on holy living and godliness. They also need to be trained to take responsibilities and leadership.

Apparently, this is precisely what Paul had done with the Ephesian elders. His entire ministry was Word-centered. That is, he did not manipulate the congregation at Ephesus by the power of his own personality, but rather taught them skillfully and carefully from the Word of God. It was a balanced ministry that emphasized both evangelism and edification. How we need to emulate this kind of balance in the Church of our day! Henry Jacobsen reminds us:

> Preachers and teachers are sometimes tempted to "ride hobbies" instead of giving their people a "balanced diet." One minister preached through the Revelation three times in eight years. Some teachers sound as though the Holy Spirit were the only really important doctrine in Scripture. Or a church emphasizes evangelism at the expense of the spiritual development of believers. Another congregation may seldom hear an evangelistic message. One church treats foreign missions as if nothing else mattered; in another all one hears about is the youth work.[2]

So Paul was not only a servant of the Lord, but also a servant of the Word. He declared the entire counsel of God, explaining from the Old Testament as well as from early New Testament traditions how Christ was the Lord of the Church.

Servant of Others

Now Paul turns the hard stare of responsibility upon the Ephesian elders. What *he* had done in the past *they* were to do now. It would require a careful guarding of themselves, as well as care over the flock. As Jesus was a Shepherd, so they were to be shepherds—overseers of the work at Ephesus.

The danger was not only from external infiltration, but also from internal perversion. Heresy would arise because people would distort God's truth and Paul's teaching. But they had been warned that these things were impending, and the warning should help them ward off the attacks of Satan.

All of this was a final message of leadership to men who would have great responsibility in a great church. He commended them "to God, and to the word of his grace, which is able to build you up, and to give you an inheritance among all them which are sanctified" (Acts 20:32).

It was an emotional moment–not unlike the moment of any leader leaving his church or ministry for the last time. But the crucial part of the passage is not that they were sorry to see Paul go or that there was grief because of the possibility of his death. The point is that the work must go on even though the worker leaves. Whether we look at Barnabas, Silas, Luke, Timothy, Epaphroditus, or the Ephesian elders, we see this amazing apostle, Paul, always concerned with transferring the mantle of leadership to others.

What a lesson this is for Sunday school superintendents and pastors in our day! We best serve others by teaching them to serve God. The need for an edificational ministry in today's church is at least as great as it was in Paul's day. The church at Ephesus became one of the stronger congregations of the first century largely because of Paul's teaching ministry among the believers there. We should never underestimate the dynamic of the church's educational program in contributing to the kind of congregational life the Bible calls for.

Paul: Communicating to Contemporary Culture

Athens was the cultural splendor of the first-century world. Though Greek philosophy and its ideals of democracy had degenerated shamefully since the days of Socrates, Plato, and Aristotle, in Paul's day the city still represented the epitome of sophistication—like a combination of Vienna, Paris, Rome, and New York at the foot of Mount Olympus.

"How different from Jerusalem!"—Paul must have thought as he sat in the marketplace watching the people. Athens must have appealed to the alert mind of the apostle, as Jerusalem with its ancient religious heritage appealed to his spirit. Perhaps throughout all history, Athens and Jerusalem will represent the natural and spiritual parts of man and will, therefore, always provide us with fodder for argument regarding the relationship of the Christian leader to the pagan culture around him.

Just a little more than two centuries after Paul walked the agora (marketplace) in ancient Athens, Christianity was legalized in the Roman Empire; and the church was allowed to enter the world without fear of physical reprisal. But the world also entered the church, and the escape from culture began. Through the Middle Ages, it took concrete form in the erection of vast monasteries, where hooded figures prayed in halls to escape the contamination of the barbarian society beyond the walls of their compounds.

Society's contamination could not reach them in their seclusion. Of course, by the same token, they could not reach society.

Monasticism continues to the present day as the historic ultimate in separationism, and the monastic mentality lingers into this last quarter of the twentieth century. It may not often take the form of seclusion centers, though modern-day examples are available. But it does frequently emerge as a mind-set or life-style in which the Christian shuns all relationship with the culture, opting to live his life "out of the world."

Jesus prayed that the Father would not take His children out of the world, but rather leave them in it to communicate the message of the cross to contemporary culture in every age (see John 17:15).

Observation or Confrontation?

Acts 17:16 is most descriptive: "Now while Paul waited for them at Athens, his spirit was stirred in him, when he saw the city wholly given to idolatry." Imagine the thoughts in his mind on that day as he watched the hundreds of busy people active in the marketplace and recalled the glories of the Athens of the past, before Rome had cut the heart out of the Greek republic. Emil G. Kraeling expresses it succinctly in the *Rand McNally Bible Atlas:*

> Athens had a glamor second to none of the Western World cities because of its poets, its thinkers, its artists, and more anciently, its lawgivers and soldiers. But it had fallen from its once proud pedestal. It was like Vienna of today—a city with a great past but with a sorry present. Rob a people of its power and wealth, and

its culture must inevitably decline. This was what Rome had been to the Greeks, and all the benefactions of its Caesars could not halt the downward trend.[1]

How long could Paul sit there watching and listening? How long can the thinking Christian observe the deterioration of culture around him before he is thrust into a confrontation with the pagan domination of the culture?

For Paul, it may have been only a matter of hours. In typical fashion, he began at the synagogue—but was soon out in the public, confronting the culture with the only message that could bring it real life! To be sure, like the Christian leader of today, he was immediately met with sophisticated pagan opposition. It was a negative climate, and the minority voice of a thinking Christian was no more welcome in Athens than it is today on the campus of a liberal state university.

But Paul had a burning passion to communicate, which was one of the most important ingredients of his leadership. Sensing that they were dealing with no ordinary intellect, the Epicureans and Stoics hustled him off to the Areopagus.

Cultural Negation or Thorough Education?

There he stood—a lonely Christian leader in an alien setting, expected to give reasonable answers in defense of the faith within him. The result was one of the most classic apologetics for the Gospel the world has ever heard!

Yet Paul has been criticized by many for the way he handled his task on that day. He neither negated the Greek culture nor attacked its validity. Rather, he called upon an amazing educational background in Greek philosophy, poetry, and religion, blended with a thorough competence in both Old Testament and Christian theology. It was a beautiful demonstration of the integration of faith and learning. In a journal article, I once pointed out that Paul did not "cop out" on the Gospel in Athens:

> Verses 31 and 32 firmly testify to evangelical witness. Paul argues that man cannot continue in idolatry overlooking God's com-

> mands because there will be a day of universal righteous judgment which has been guaranteed by the resurrection of Jesus Christ. Christ is to be the Judge, and the destiny of redeemed man is fellowship with God through repentance and faith in the resurrection.[2]

Paul's leadership in Athens argues for a thorough *general* as well as *theological* education for those who would lead Christ's Church in our day. If anything, naturalism and humanism are more rampant in the major cultural centers of the world today than they were in the first century. Paul gave Christ everything he had, including his mind. Dare we offer any less?

Separation or Communication?

What should Paul say to this gathering of pagan philosophers? Should he proclaim a historical accounting of how Jehovah has dealt with His people throughout the days of their nationhood, culminating in His final revelation, Jesus Christ? That was an excellent message for the Jewish accusers to whom Stephen spoke, but it would have been nonsense for the Greek philosophers.

Paul recognized that *a central responsibility of leadership is communication* and that communication requires understanding; so he began where his listeners could identify with what he was saying–the worship of an unknown god. As Longenecker puts it: "He was prepared to correct and instruct his converts by beginning at a point of common agreement, and then leading them on to an appreciation of rightful significance in and proper expression of their Christian faith."[3]

There were converts at Athens. Not many, but enough to show that the Gospel had indeed been preached there and that Paul had communicated the truth of God's revelation to a city in which such a message was completely unknown.

But did Paul compromise a biblical position on separation in the process? I think not. Perhaps some would have Paul ignoring the Athenian philosophers completely or maybe handing them a tract or inviting them to his synagogue lecture. Paul demonstrated a unique sensitivity to the communications context by dealing with the semantic problem (words), the emotional problem (feelings), and the environmental problem (attitudes) of his hostile listeners.

Isolation or Penetration?

Ultimately, this is the question that faces Christian leadership in our day. Shall we withdraw behind the safe walls of our churches and schools, letting the culture drift toward a Christless eternity? Is isolation the answer? Can we insulate children, young people, and adults so that they are virtually immune to—or at least unreachable by—the devastating effects of their barbarian surroundings?

That certainly does not seem to be the New Testament pattern. The Church of the first century carried the Gospel into the world. It invaded home and synagogue, marketplace and palace. It made the message of Jesus Christ a viable and rational alternative to the prevailing philosophies of the moment. And, as it had done to Jesus Christ, Athens rejected the apostle. In his brilliant biography, John Pollock puts it this way:

> He could not know that his speech would go down to posterity beside the Funeral Oration of Pericles and the Philippics of Demosthenes as one of the great speeches of Athens. He could not know that whole books would be written about it or that in a few hundred years the Parthenon would become a Christian church; and that nineteen centuries on, when Greece after long suppression became once more a sovereign state, the national flag which flies beside the ruins of the Parthenon would be lowered to half mast each good Friday and raised on Easter day in honor of Christ's resurrection.[4]

But let us not think only in terms of history. The real issue that faces us is the lesson in leadership that Paul gave us that day on the Areopagus. We must also communicate to contemporary culture, and the call issued almost a decade ago in the article mentioned above continues to the present hour:

The intelligentsia of American society today have not been offered by contemporary Christianity as distinctive a witness to truth as that heard by the Greek philosophers in Athens on that day. The "preaching of the cross" does not have to consist of simplistic verbal meandering calculated to evoke appropriate emotional responses. The Areopagus sermon offers us a standard of excellence in depth and relevance. Let the modern-day Athenians hear again the words of the risen Christ.

Timothy: Quality Control in Leadership

20

One of the exciting things about reading the New Testament is its constant relevance to our times. Sometimes it is difficult to grasp the fact that the Scriptures were written thousands of years ago, so much impact do they have in our society today. Perhaps it is because the pagan culture of the last quarter of the twentieth century is not unlike the pagan culture of the last quarter of the first century. Someone has suggested that being a Christian in our time is more like being a Christian in New Testament times than in any other era in between.

The opening verses of the fourth chapter of 1 Timothy clearly identify the difficulties that the Church will experience in the end times. The Bible warns us that "some shall depart from the faith, giving heed to seducing spirits, and doctrines of devils; speaking lies in hypocrisy; having their conscience seared with a hot iron" (vv. 1-2). Legalism will prevail. Pharisaism, instead of brotherhood, will characterize even the Church, and believer will fight with believer over petty things such as what should or should not be eaten by Christians.

In the midst of this kind of confusion and apostasy, God still calls men and women to serve as leaders; and He expects them to maintain a level of excellence, a quality control, a consistent spiritual tone in the organizations over which He has given them supervision.

What kind of leadership will it take to produce such an atmosphere? What kind of people are required to serve the Church in the latter days and retain its purity and witness in the world when the situation all around seems so dark?

A number of the qualifications for leadership have been identified in 1 Timothy 3. We can assume that God was speaking to Timothy through Paul about leaders who are called to their particular posts, who have not grasped or usurped leadership outside the will of God. Spiritual maturity was also assumed as Paul went on to identify, in the rest of chapter 4, something of the kind of leadership Timothy had to maintain if he was going to serve the church effectively in days of apostasy.

Alert Leadership

In the sixth verse of 1 Timothy 4, the apostle describes a "good minister of Jesus Christ" as one who is progressive and yet conservative. Normally, we think of those terms as antonyms; but in reality, in almost any leadership situation there are some things which should be changed and some things which should be retained. The wise and balanced administrator will be able to understand those areas in which he should be progressive—that is, moving ahead with change and innovation; and those areas in which he should be conservative, maintaining the values of tradition and the past.

That is why I have chosen the word "alert" to describe this kind of leadership. In order to be that good minister, Timothy needed to understand the people he was working with, understand the information they needed to know, and have a keen alertness to the times around him. In other words, the sharp leader understands the culture in which his leadership must take place. He is a student of society as well as a student of Scripture. It is certainly not an emphasis on one to the exclusion of the other because after talking about the nature of society in the first five verses of the chapter, Paul reminded Timothy, at the end of 1 Timothy 4:6, that he must also be a man "nourished up in the words of faith and of good doctrine, whereunto thou has attained."

Godly Leadership

The way one attains godliness in leadership is through rigorous self-discipline (see 1 Tim. 4:7-8). The Authorized Version uses the words "exercise thyself . . . unto godliness." The New International Version says "train yourself." Other versions offer the same emphasis, which clearly has to do with the same type of rigorous training that must be utilized by an athlete to prepare himself in conditioning for satisfactory achievement in his selected sport.

Be careful not to downgrade the mention of the physical here, for the intent of the passage is a comparison, not a negation of one to the exaltation of the other. Paul was not saying that physical exercise is of no value and that you should spend all your time reading the Bible. Rather, he was saying that physical exercise is of value, and I presume that he anticipated Timothy would take care of the physical temple which houses the Spirit of God, making possible his leadership.

But if it ever comes to a question of priorities in which one must make a choice of the physical or the spiritual, Paul wanted Timothy to know that the spiritual is clearly the more important in godly leadership. Christian colleges and seminaries would do well to remind their faculty and students that physical discipline is important for the Christian leader, as is spiritual discipline.

The analogy is unmistakable. Just as physical discipline

provides value for the temporal body, spiritual discipline not only provides benefits now, while we exist in physical form, but is also of eternal value. It serves also the life "which is to come" (1 Tim. 4:8).

Sacrificial Leadership

The Christian leader is to follow in the footsteps of his Lord, which will lead him to a position of reproach and perhaps even suffering (see 1 Tim. 4:9-10). In some cases, it may even lead to death. After Timothy had labored to carry out his leadership tasks successfully, he could not assume that everyone would applaud his efforts and reward him appropriately. He was to put his trust in a loving God and anticipate eternal rewards for the sacrificial nature of the leadership role.

Exemplary Leadership

The verbal responsibility of leadership is clear in the brief wording of 1 Timothy 4:11, "These things command and teach." The leader has the responsibility to take charge (within the bounds of cooperative ministry) and to teach. But we may assume from verse 12 that all verbal leadership will come to naught unless it is also supported by the life-modeling system which was made famous by the Apostle Paul patterned after the Lord Jesus.

Unfortunately, verse 12 is sometimes used to encourage teen-agers—and I suppose we should rejoice, if the results are positive. But in true interpretation of the context, most reputable commentators believe that Timothy was well into his thirties by the time these words were written. That would have been very young for an elder in the first-century church. Paul wanted Timothy to overcome the hindrance of age by demonstrating spiritual maturity.

Age is not a calculator of spiritual maturity. A person who is 25 or 30 years old could very well be more grown up in spiritual things than a person who is 40 or 50. Maturity comes from experience. The person who has engaged in serious Bible study, fervent and persevering prayer, and active Christian service will build spiritual maturity, whereas the person who has been slothful about these important areas will stay a babe in Christ regardless of his physical development or chronological age.

Notice the key areas in which Timothy was to express the exemplary life of leadership: language, behavior, love, spirit, faith, and purity or holiness. This is a heavy demand to lay upon a young man, but no less a biblical responsibility therefore.

Communicative Leadership

A leader must take in before he can give out. So Paul said to Timothy, "Don't neglect your reading, so that your exhortation means something on the basis of a well-developed doctrine" (1 Tim. 4:13 lit. trans.). Timothy was to give his congregation meat, and not milk. His sermons were to come from the garden, not from the barrel. Oh, how Christian leaders in our day need to hear again the resounding voice of the great apostle: "Give attendance to reading."

Communication with his co-workers is extremely important for a leader in any situation, and it is certainly true within the context of the church. Paul recognized that, and wanted to make sure that Timothy not only knew *how* to say, but also that he had something to say when he addressed his congregation.

Gifted Leadership

It is very difficult to be dogmatic about the exact interpretation of 1 Timothy 4:14. What spiritual gift is in view here? Exactly how did Timothy get it? Are spiritual gifts still given by "the laying on of the hands of the presbytery"? Several hermeneutical options are possible. It could very well have been the gift of prophecy itself, whereby Timothy explained and applied the written Word of God from the Old Testament and whatever fragments of the New Testament were already available to him.

On the other hand, it could have been the gift of pastoral ministry, which he was to exercise among the churches over which he had responsibility. Perhaps it was the gift of teaching, since in another passage Paul reminded Timothy that teaching would be part of his responsibility as well. Whatever the gift, the emphasis is on a recognition of the gift and a willingness to develop it and use it for the glory of Christ and in the power of the Holy Spirit. The neglect of a spiritual gift is like the atrophy of a muscle. It may still be there, but it is of little use unless it has been exercised and developed properly.

Persevering Leadership

Leadership, for Timothy, was to be a complete commitment. Paul had outlined several things which were important, and Timothy was to "meditate upon these things" and give himself wholly to them (1 Tim. 4:15). No halfway job, no incompetence, no slothfulness or laziness would be permitted. Christian leadership is serious business, and Paul wanted Timothy to clearly understand that he must pay the price if he was going to do the job in the name of Jesus Christ.

Not only that, but his main problem was not going to be other people, but himself! The doctrine was important, but his own personal spiritual life before God was more important. What an ugly thing it is to see a Christian leader who argues vehemently for pure doctrine while exhibiting a life of bitterness and hostility toward other Christians. This leader, by his very behavior, denies the love that marks the true Christian.

In the final words of 1 Timothy 4, Paul reminds Timothy that persevering leadership is not only beneficial to the leader himself, but also will bring great value to those he serves. Leadership is never done in isolation; it is always a group-oriented activity.

In our particular situations, the words "them that hear thee" (1 Tim. 4:16) may apply to a small Sunday school class or a congregation of thousands, but the principle is the same. What we *are* before God as leaders is more important than what we *do* or *say*. When what we *are* is in line with God's requirements, then what we do and say will fall into place because of His Spirit's control.

21
Epaphras: Hometown Boy Makes Good

It has been said that God can use "nobodies" to accomplish His work. Epaphras certainly seems to fall into that category. He is hardly one of the outstanding heroes of the New Testament and is mentioned only briefly in the Book of Colossians (see 1:7; 4:12-13).

His name probably is a contraction of the longer name "Epaphroditus," but he is not to be confused with the messenger delegated by the church at Philippi to bring their gifts to Paul while the apostle was in prison. Some suggest that Epaphras may have been the founder of the church at Colossae, and he certainly was a special delegate to the church, sent from his mentor, the Apostle Paul. Indeed, we are led to think that he may have made frequent visits between the apostle and the church, carrying messages both ways.

The thing that impresses me most about Epaphras—the reason I decided to include him in this book on leadership—is his *close identification with the work of the local church.* We live in a day when Christian leaders seem to find avenues of leadership and time consumption in endless para-church activities, sometimes to the detriment of their own local congregations.

To be sure, most of these activities are extremely worthy, and the service of God's people is needed to keep their ministries effective. But the man who loses contact with his local church and fails to serve Jesus Christ there will soon find himself estranged from God's family and attempting to carry out a ministry that majors on minors while ignoring God's priorities.

Priority of Leadership Development

One cannot think about Epaphras without thinking about both Paul and the church at Colossae. The brilliant Greek Scholar J. B. Lightfoot spends 72 pages in his excellent commentary reviewing the geographical, cultural, and religious setting of "the churches of the Lycus." Describing the town of Epaphras' home church, he reminds us that:

> The site of Colossae is somewhat higher up the stream, at a distance of perhaps ten or twelve miles from the point where the road between Laodicea and Hierapolis crosses the Lycus. Unlike Laodicea and Hierapolis, which overhang the valley on opposite sides, Colossae stands immediately on the riverbank, the two parts of the town being divided by the stream. The three cities lie so near to each other that it would be quite possible to visit them all in the course of a single day.[1]

Lightfoot believes that Paul had never visited the church at Colossae at the time of the writing of this epistle and perhaps never had that opportunity in his entire life. He, rather, takes the view that Epaphras was the originator of the church, and expresses it this way:

> By Epaphras they had been converted to the gospel. This is the evident meaning of a passage in the opening of the epistle, which has been much obscured by misreading and mistranslation, and which may be paraphrased thus: "The gospel which has spread and borne throughout the rest of the world, has been equally successful among yourselves. This fertile growth has been manifested

in you the first day when the message of God's grace was preached to you and accepted by you—preached not as now with adulteration by these false teachers, but in its genuine simplicity by Epaphras our beloved fellow servant; he has been a faithful minister of Christ and a faithful representative of us, and from him we have received tidings of your love in the Spirit."[2]

It is my view that Epaphras may very well have been a native product of the region, sent back by Paul to minister at Colossae. Though it could certainly not be said that he "grew up in the church," one must conclude that it became his home church and the one to which he was specifically assigned by the apostle.

The spotlight here rests on Paul's ability to train people just like Epaphras to do precisely what Epaphras did in the ministry of Christ. Apparently, his task was largely that of evangelist-pastor, and the characteristics of his ministry were faithfulness and durability.

The very significant Greek term *doulos* (bond-slave) is used in the New Testament by Paul only of himself and once of Timothy in Philippians 1:1. But it is also used of this little-known young man, Epaphras, in the twelfth verse of Colossians 4. Like Paul and Timothy, whose fame in the New Testament spread far beyond his own, Epaphras was a true "servant of Christ."

Prayer as a Mark of Leadership

Epaphras not only ministered on location at Colossae, but when he was out of the city he also labored consistently and fervently for his people in prayer. His goal was their spiritual maturity, and he prayed that they might "stand perfect and complete in all the will of God" (Col. 4:12). One of the characteristics of all the great leaders of both Old and New Testaments is their willingness to pray for the people they lead. Yet, in the complex and harried society of our day, how difficult it seems to be for us to find the time—or to *make* the time—to genuinely pray for those for whom we have responsibility.

Every pastor, Sunday school superintendent, and church leader should have a prayer list from which he regularly appeals to God for those who serve with him and under his leadership in the work of the ministry.

The church, in turn, ought to be consistently praying that many of its young people will become like Epaphras. I have always been impressed with that simple phrase at the beginning of Colossians 4:12, "who is one of you." Epaphras was not an outsider foisted upon the region of the Lycus Valley but, I take it, a hometown boy who returned with the Gospel.

Practicality of Short-Term Service

Leadership development can be carried on in a number of different ways, but one of the best ways is to get a potential leader on the field exercising leadership for a period of time. I have no idea how closely this ties in with the experience of Epaphras, but it is a technique which the Apostle Paul used frequently with many of his disciples—and perhaps it was applied in Epaphras' case as well.

There are ample opportunities now for the young people of the church to spend time in other countries or in different sections of their own country serving Jesus Christ and learning leadership.

Perhaps the most obvious product of such a trip is spiritual maturity—learning how to be a man or a woman of God, rather than a little boy or girl constantly displaying the marks of immaturity. From such short-term service experiences, the potential leader benefits, the church benefits, the mission board or ministry which was served for that period of time benefits, and in the final analysis, the total work of Jesus Christ is furthered.

Productivity—A Measure of Church Health

What is the best way to judge a healthy church? By its size? Without question, that is the easiest and most popular way of measuring the quality of a local congregation. For Americans, "big equals good." But, of course, that is never identified as a criterion in the New Testament, and after the initial specification of numbers in the Book of Acts, we have no idea whether the church at Ephesus was large or small or whether the church at Colossae was bigger than the churches at Ephesus and Philippi.

One thing does emerge in the New Testament, especially in this young man Epaphras–productivity. Local churches should be producing Christian workers at a respectable rate. To be very specific, the pastor who has ministered in a certain church, let us say, 10 years, should be able to look back on growth in the size of the membership and, of course, spiritual growth in all of the people. But he should also be able to identify young people who have responded to God's call to Christian service and are presently serving the Lord at home or abroad.

Again, I need to clarify that Epaphras is not an exact example of this principle. He may have been raised in the area of Colossae, but there was no church there during his childhood and teen years; so he could not be said to be a product of the Colossian congregation. But we do take seriously that point of his return to his own home area as Christ's servant.

In speaking about Epaphras' concern for his church, A. T. Robertson writes:

> Epaphras evidently took the Gnostic peril seriously and was wrestling with God constantly that they might stand firm against the wiles of these plausible deceivers. Meanwhile, he was appealing to Paul also to help him get the answer to his prayers. This confidence rests "in everything willed by God," which is more exact than "in all the will of God."[3]

Privilege of Training Leaders

Paul's joy in Christ came from both the behavior and response of the Colossian believers and the activity of his young student in their midst. I can imagine that the Colossian believers also responded most favorably toward the ministry of Epaphras. There is a privilege in training leaders that belongs to the local church, to individual Christian leaders who reproduce after their own kind, and to Christian schools at all levels.

One of the problems the American church has always faced is that it has not taken seriously enough its mandate from God to pray that the Lord of the harvest will call forth laborers into His harvest and then to create situations in which those harvesters can be properly trained.

With every privilege comes a commensurate responsibility. Even in times of lean financial resources, the church dare not turn away from the production of young men like Epaphras who will accept the responsibility before God for the care of some arena of Christian ministry.

Who is the future Epaphras in your church? How can you encourage him to consider God's call to some form of Christian ministry? Of course, you are not the Holy Spirit, nor do you want to lead a young person in a direction that God does not want him to go. But isn't it possible that he has not been honestly confronted with the option of taking responsibility for a portion of the church, as did Epaphras?

Perhaps an encouraging word from you, his parent, teacher or pastor, is just what is needed. God may want you, like Paul, to be the one who pours years of his life into the structuring of another life of leadership just like your own.

Philemon: Serving Christ at Home

The Book of Philemon is the only definitely private letter of all of Paul's writings, which has been preserved. To be sure, the books of Titus and Timothy are addressed to individuals, but they obviously contain material which related to the total church and were intended from the outset to be used as books of church doctrine and practice. The letter to Philemon, however, does not deal with any public issues, but specifically with an incident in the domestic life of a Christian layman.

In many ways, it is a social statement, because it contains the largest treatment of the issue of slavery we find anywhere in the Bible. Of course, it is not a cry for justice or a declaration of equality, but rather a simple appeal for mercy written from friend to friend.

But if we get too deeply into the social implications of the Book of Philemon, we shall miss the point of this particular article. To be sure, there is much to be learned from a focus on Onesimus and the conditions of the letter. But it is my purpose to emphasize the role of Philemon, not so much as slave-owner and friend of the apostle, but rather as a Christian layman of middle-class credentials who was serving Christ to the best of his abilities at home.

Raising a Godly Family

Philemon was one leader in the New Testament who understood that leadership begins at home. This is the message which rings through the pages of the Bible from the stories of the patriarchs, through the sad tale of Eli, to the specific conditions for elders and deacons laid down by Paul in the third chapter of the Book of 1 Timothy. Quite obviously, Philemon was a native (or at least a resident) of Colossae, and probably a convert of the Apostle Paul (see Philemon 19).

Philemon had apparently made his home available for the gathering of the Christians at Colossae. He had learned the Christian grace of hospitality, and apparently all those with whom he came in contact spoke with gratitude of things he did for them. Verse 5 is particularly notable in thinking through Philemon's reputation: "Hearing of thy love and faith, which thou hast toward the Lord Jesus, and toward all saints."

Love is a characteristic of discipleship described in John 13:35; and faith, or trust, represents both a gift and a fruit of the Spirit. Quite a tribute to Philemon's life style is offered here—and it is not a simple accolade from the writer of the epistle, but rather the attitude of the townspeople toward this outstanding Christian layman.

The second member of the family was Philemon's wife, Apphia. We really know nothing more about "Mrs. Philemon" than we learn in this epistle. Presumably, she was also a believer. Although she may not have shared leadership with her husband on as dominant a plane as was exhibited by Aquila and Priscilla, she apparently was sufficiently concerned with the situation which occasioned the letter to warrant mention by Paul at its beginning.

We may assume that Archippus was the son of Philemon and Apphia. Far from being some kind of spoiled brat in a wealthy home, Archippus is referred to as Paul's fellow soldier. He is also mentioned in Colossians 4:17 as holding some important office in the church at Colossae. Possibly he was an evangelist in the area, or perhaps even a deacon at the church which met in his parents' home. Some commentators connect Archippus with Laodicea, since that church would have been within walking distance of his hometown of Colossae.

Such was Philemon's household—with the exception, of course, of Onesimus, who had run away. We will come to him in just a moment. Suffice it here to emphasize that the three members of the household had probably not been offensive to their young slave. Indeed, one can imagine that they may have attempted on numerous occasions to lead him to Christ so that he might share the family's faith and hope.

There are few enough examples of a truly godly family in the pages of Scripture, and we should not overlook the importance of this one in the early verses of the Book of Philemon.

Serving a Local Church

I have already commented on the reputation of Philemon in his own town, but the second section of the epistle goes beyond just the reputation of what Philemon was. It also describes what he did to forward the work of Christ at the local level. He was actively communicating his faith. Paul commended Philemon, telling him: "I pray that you may be active in sharing your faith, so that you will have a full understanding. . . ." The effectiveness of Philemon's outer communication in the church and the world would help to secure his internal recognition ". . . of every good thing we have in Christ" (Philemon 6 NIV).

An effective Christian layman serving willingly and humbly in a local church (whether it is in his own home or not) will invariably bring joy to others. In this case, Philemon was a source of joy to the missionary, to the local church, to the entire program of the Lord's work in his area, and obviously to the Lord Himself. Philemon 7 is translated in the New International Version in this fashion: "Your love has given me great joy and encouragement, because you, brother, have refreshed the hearts of the saints." How prophetic Philemon's parents were in assigning him a name which is taken from the Greek verb *phileo,* meaning "to love"!

So Philemon was not only active in a local church, but he actually hosted that local church in his own home. This was a practice not at all uncommon in the first century. E. M. Blaiklock writes:

> It is to be noted that the Christian community was organized around a home, a practice of the early church. Many ancient churches were no doubt founded on the sites of homes where early Christians met. There is no evidence of church-building of any sort before the third century.[1]

Facing a Social Problem

The subject matter of the letter is an unpleasant one for both writer and reader. We can only produce conjecture regarding what type of turmoil the pagan slave may have created in the household of his Christian owner. True, there was frustration, perplexity, and no little prayer regarding the situation. Paul assumed, probably correctly, that Philemon would have the authority, as well as the tendency, to discipline Onesimus if he were found and returned to his master.

Living in our day, and particularly in our culture, we can certainly understand this epistle in the light of its own time and social context. It is most interesting that before the incident in Philemon's household, which probably took place sometime in the mid-60s of the first century, the name "Onesimus" was commonly used for slaves.

After the writing of this Pauline epistle, however, the name gained enormous popularity among Christians and was used quite widely across Asia Minor for children, and even taken by influential church leaders such as bishops. J. B. Lightfoot properly assesses the situation:

> Onesimus represented the least respectable type of the least respectable class in the social scale. He was regarded by philosophers as "live chattel," a "live implement"; and he had taken philosophy at her word. He had done what a chattel or an implement might be expected to do, if endued with life and intelligence. He was treated by the law as having no rights, and he had carried the principles of the law to their logical consequences. He had declined to entertain any responsibilities. There was absolutely nothing to recommend him. . . . He was a thief and a runaway. . . . He had packed up some goods and taken to his heels. Rome was the natural cesspool for these off-scourings of humanity. In the throngs of the metropolis was his best hope of secrecy. In the dregs of the city rabble he would find the society of congenial spirits.[2]

Responding to a Colleague

We can only speculate how Philemon responded to Paul's letter. I believe it was with enthusiastic affirmation. What a thrill it would be to know that a member of his household, the lowest slave, had now become a brother in Christ! What a joyous reunion it must have been when Onesimus returned to Colossae!

The Christian answer to social problems, now as then, is never anarchy or violence. It is not even passive resistance which takes some illegal form. It is, rather, a constant encouraging of other Christians and even the pagan society itself to adopt Christian ideas of brotherhood and equality which transcend classes and unite people across social boundaries and cultural dividing lines.

Paul typically aligned the new convert with himself. How could Philemon turn down a letter like this? Paul simply said: "If you would welcome me at your house, please welcome Onesimus in the same way. If you think he owes you anything, I will pay it the next time I see you" (Philemon 18-19 lit. trans.). Grace for grace and substitutionary involvement—that's the key to serving Christ at home or anywhere else! Of course, Paul was always the Jewish diplomat, and he reminded Philemon that his very eternal salvation was dependent on Paul's willingness to share the Gospel (see Philemon 19).

Perhaps Paul's dealings with Philemon represent for us an ideal picture of human relations in Christian leadership. A power-mad society claws itself to death in a dog-eat-dog struggle for control of other people. Rampant manipulation passes for motivation even in Christian organizations, as the politics of power overshadow the gospel of love.

But Paul knew that church leadership was to be different. Like his Lord before him, the apostle displayed a consistent spirit of meekness and submission, even to men like Philemon—with whom he could have "pulled rank." The real slave of this epistle is Paul—a *doulos* (bond-slave) to Jesus Christ and, for His sake, servant to the members of God's family.

So "responding to a colleague" becomes the test of the metal, the mark of the Christian, as Francis Schaeffer has reminded us. And Paul offers us an example in this little letter which has survived the test of time. An epistle on social justice? Not really. The Book of Philemon is rather a model of Christian behavior—the assumed loving response of Philemon, as well as the gracious request of Paul.

And Paul knew his friend. Philemon would not only receive Onesimus, he would do more than Paul requested. The picture is beautiful: a layman and his faith serving Christ and the church—at home.

John: A Leader Grows Old Gracefully

Long life has always been a goal of human society, and statistics indicate that Western nations, toward the end of the twentieth century, may be at last achieving that goal. Because of the population explosion and better medical care, it has been reasonably estimated that half of all people who have ever lived to the age of 65 are still living today. Sociologist David O. Moberg offers the following statistics:

> As of 1 July 1966, there were approximately 18,457,000 people age 60-65 and over in the United States and nearly eight million additional persons aged 60-64. In other words, almost one-tenth of the national population has passed the age of 65, and 13.4 percent are aged 60 and over. In many local communities the proportions are substantially higher. Numerous Midwestern villages are almost like retirement communities because of their heavy concentrations of elderly people. The net increase of the population past age 65 is 820 per day. By 1985, they are expected to total more than 25,000,000.[1]

Moberg's estimates, which were written more than five

years ago, have proved, if anything, to be conservative. Dealing with the elderly in North American society has become a major concern—not only for the church, but for civil government as well.

The amazing thing is that we have seen the increasing mass of elderly persons only as a problem, and not as a blessing. Rarely do we talk about the rich resource which they present to a culture. Churches have designed few, if any, programs to take advantage of the contributions senior citizens can make to the ministry of Christ and His Church in this confusing age.

It was not always so in the Church. There was a time when the accumulated insight of age was deemed of great merit, and Bible writers like the Apostle John proudly referred to themselves as "elders." In his little paperback commentary on the Johannine epistles, E. M. Blaiklock describes the kind of man behind that magnificent first epistle:

> We find more than history there. We find the author. To gain some notion of the mind of one who walked with Christ half a century beyond those momentous days, is fascinatingly interesting. We know little of the Apostle's life over those fifty years but enough perhaps to follow its main outlines. Several references in Acts and one in Galatians suggest he remained in Jerusalem until about A.D. 50. It is possible that he was in Rome at the time of Nero's cruel persecution of the middle 60s and probable that, after the martyrdom of Peter and Paul, he went to Ephesus. His mature ministry was certainly exercised here. The seven churches of Revelation were no doubt his "circuit." Revelation itself was written during this period.[2]

Perhaps in examining the contribution of this great aged apostle to the Church of *his* day, we can learn something about what senior citizens of *our* day can provide to help meet the leadership needs of local congregations. Then we cannot only minister to their needs, but must also allow them to minister to the wider Body of Christ, utilizing the gifts and abilities that God has given to them.

Knowledge

John lived to be about 100 years of age, by far the oldest of the apostles who intimately walked with the Lord. During that time, he developed an enormous storehouse of knowledge about the truth of God. Indeed, William Sanford LaSor suggests that John was called at Ephesus "the Holy Theologian," and adds that "the Theologian, therefore, should have a long life, for he has many observations to make; he should be intimately acquainted with God, not only in mystical immediacy but also in some way that is sensuously verifiable; and he should be gifted in ability to make known his conclusions in such a way that others will understand him."[3]

One of the key words of John's first epistle is the Greek word *oida,* which means "to know." Sample verses appear in the text, as in 2:20-21: "But ye have an unction from the Holy One, and ye know all things. I have not written unto you because ye know not the truth, but because ye know it, and that no lie is of the truth."

Growing old gracefully in leadership means not only having knowledge, but also being willing to share it with others. Our senior citizens cannot do that unless we show a willingness to listen and an eagerness to learn. We need to be like the "little children" to whom John wrote, even though some of them were clearly fathers and young men (see 1 John 2:13).

Wisdom

Someone has said that wisdom is the ability to put knowledge into practice. In one of my books I deal with the gift of wisdom and come to a similar conclusion.

> Wisdom can be accumulated through experience, but this is not true of the "utterance of wisdom" which marks the spiritual gift. As with all spiritual gifts, the gift of wisdom is supernatural, focusing on the meaning or interpretation of truth, producing understanding of solutions to some problem, or offering the ap-

plication of knowledge to spiritual life.[4]

Not all elderly persons have the gift of wisdom, as no doubt John did—but all do have that kind of wisdom which is accumulated through experience.

In a pressure-cooker society which produces strange ideas about as fast as a popcorn popper explodes the kernels, we have a desperate need for the leveling influence of wisdom. To be sure, very young persons can have the gift of wisdom and even accumulate experiential wisdom. But one is more likely to find it among the elders, or at least that seems to be the general tone of the New Testament. John was a veteran, a senior, the veritable patriarch of his age. Of him, John R. W. Stott writes:

> We conclude, therefore, that although we can only guess how and why the writer came to be called "the elder" in his anonymous and absolute way, the use of the title tends to confirm the unique position of the person who held it. Such an exceptional position, together with the author's authoritative tone and claim to be an eyewitness, are fully consistent with the early tradition of the Church that these three Epistles were, in fact, written by the Apostle John.[5]

Spirit of Unity

John made much of the concept of fellowship, and identified the obtaining of both vertical and horizontal fellowship as one of the purposes of his first epistle (see 1:3-4). Out of his concern that Christians be able to relate satisfactorily to one another comes a strong emphasis on love, another one of the key words in the first epistle. Over and over again, he reminds us: "We know that we have passed from death unto life, because we love the brethren" (3:14). And again: "My little children, let us not love in word, neither in tongue; but in deed and in truth. And hereby we know that we are of the truth, and shall assure our hearts before him" (vv. 18-19).

Though I have no statistics readily at hand, my guess would be that most church splits are not precipitated by senior citizens. They have seen the storms of life and prefer to keep the waters calm, promoting a general spirit of unity in the congregation. Obviously, there may be notorious exceptions to this general rule; but if we take John as a model, we certainly see a very strong commitment to the unity of believers.

Here again, our elders of today can help us. They can help us through prayer, through counsel, and through providing the kind of healing oil of which the church is in constant need.

Awareness of Christ's Return

It is clearly reasonable that the older one grows in the Lord, the more dynamic the promise of Christ's return becomes. Almost all the New Testament writers speak of the Lord's return; indeed, 1 out of every 25 verses in the New Testament deals with the subject. But other than the teaching of our Lord Himself, never does it come through more clearly than in the words of Paul and John during their latter days on the earth.

John reminded the believers: "It doth not yet appear what we shall be: but we know that, when he shall appear, we shall be like him; for we shall see him as he is" (1 John 3:2). Paul and John were not afraid to die, but of far greater promise was the expectation of seeing the Lord face to face. And that hope, that constant reminder of His soon appearing, produced holiness in their lives.

One tends to believe that the same format is operative today. Older men and women in the church who eagerly wait for the return of the Lord may have a unique holiness of life that others have difficulty attaining. If so, it probably comes from that constant awareness that the Saviour could break through the skies at any moment. Having lived their lives almost to the finish, they, above all of us, stand ready and happy to see Him.

Experience

Without boasting, John never tired of reminding his readers that he walked and talked with the Lord. His first epistle begins with a clear declaration of the author's eyewitness credentials:

> That which was from the beginning, which we have heard, which we have seen with our eyes, which we have looked upon, and our hands have handled, of the Word of life; (for the life was manifested, and we have seen it, and bear witness, and shew unto you that eternal life, which was with the Father, and was manifested unto us) (1 John 1:2).

There is no way to gain experience without experiencing life. One can get knowledge from experience, but he can also get knowledge from books. One gains wisdom from experience, but he could also possess the gift of wisdom which is not essentially related to learning by doing. But the accumulated experience of years can come only by living.

We have among us, in all our churches, older men and older women. They are gifts of God to the church, who can add immeasurably to its life and ministry if only they can learn how a leader grows old gracefully and if only we can learn how to view them as potential leaders rather than as problems.

Jude: Winning Against the Odds

From the text of the Book of Jude, we know that the author was the servant of Jesus Christ and the brother of James (see v. 1). Most evangelical scholars connect the author of this book with the brother of Jesus who had denied the Lord in the earlier days of His ministry.

It is important to remember that this is a general epistle, which means that it was written to many churches in the first century as an open letter. It was not directed toward a particular church or a specific destination such as Ephesus or Galatia.

The purpose of Jude is to point out the constant, uphill battle that the Christian leader faces against apostasy within the ranks of the people of God. The book is not dealing with paganism or even Judaism, but, rather, the author wrote to warn the saints against drifting and to assure them of God's ability to keep them in the midst of apostasy.

Jude represents, in this book, the classic dilemma of the leader—even to the present age. While wanting to be positive and constructive, he was forced, because of his position of leadership, to deal with problems. In typical form, the leader has to handle what must be done, rather than what he would like to do.

Apostasy in the Early Church

> Beloved, when I gave all diligence to write unto you of the common salvation, it was needful for me to write unto you, and exhort you that ye should earnestly contend for the faith which was once delivered unto the saints. For there are certain men crept in unawares, who were before of old ordained to this condemnation, ungodly men, turning the grace of our God into lasciviousness, and denying the only Lord God, and our Lord Jesus Christ (Jude 3-4).

The matters taken up in this epistle are dealt with because of an urgency which the Holy Spirit laid upon Jude. He was clearly compelled from within to encourage the saints to earnestly agonize for the faith. The word "contend" is used only here in the New Testament, but in classical Greek it is used of athletes striving to win in the races.

These false teachers, spreading the apostasy, had sneaked in as if by a side door. Their damage was being done from within the church, rather than from without. The apostates were replacing the genuine truth of God and the biblical concept of grace with a philosophy of "free sinning" not unlike the permissiveness so evident in our day.

Apostasy in the Old Testament

> I will therefore put you in remembrance, though ye once knew this, how that the Lord, having saved the people out of the land of Egypt, afterward destroyed them that believed not. And the angels which kept not their first estate, but left their own habitation, he hath reserved in everlasting chains under darkness unto the judgment of the great day. Even as Sodom and Gomorrha, and the cities about them in like manner, giving themselves over to fornication, and going after strange flesh, are set forth for an example, suffering the vengeance of eternal fire (Jude 5-7).

In order to point up the full biblical scenario of what was happening to the church, Jude deals with three historic judgments: the judgment of the Children of Israel, the judgment of the angels that sinned, and the judgment of Sodom and Gomorrha. The first reference is obviously to the generation of grumblers who refused to believe the good reports of the spies to enter the Promised Land, and therefore died in the wilderness, never experiencing what God had for them.

The reference to the fallen angels (whether one considers it to be a reference to the original Fall or a description of angelic fornication in Genesis 6) indicates that these spirit beings are presently being carefully guarded until the final day of judgment, when their fate will be sealed eternally.

The third case, that of Sodom and Gomorrha, is most relevant for our time. Though these cities were widely known for many kinds of sin, their most dominant sin was sexual perversion in the form of homosexuality.

Yet, we are being told now, even by some religious leaders, that homosexuality is just an optional sexual life-style, not sin or perversion. And the odds are growing against a biblical position.[1] In the midst of cultural and moral breakdown, the Christian leader needs to stand rationally and intelligently against the multiple voices raised in opposition to his Christian commitment. It will be no easier for us than it was for Jude to stand against the tide, especially when the enemy comes at us from within.

Apostasy–Its Advocates Described

One could spend a great amount of time dealing with all the details in the very important passage of Jude 1:8-19. Suffice it to say that the advocates of apostasy were clearly possessed of an evil purpose right from the start. They refused to recognize true authority and honor and even spoke evil of dignitaries (see v. 8). As the angels thought lightly of God's boundaries, as Sodom mocked moral law, as Israel refused God's leading, so these apostates refused to honor God's prophets and angels, and even God Himself.

It is interesting, too, that these apostates perverted church ordinances and doctrine (see vv. 12-13). When the believers came together to eat a fellowship meal, the false teachers participated in the feasts like hidden rocks in a shallow bay.

In verses 17-19, Jude came to a stark contrast with the use of the words "But, beloved." All this was expected. The presence of apostates causing division in the church was clearly indicated by the apostles.

Perhaps the significance in the leadership of Jude at this point emerges in two forms–his teaching ministry and his courage. His teaching ministry was protective of those he led, even to the point of clarifying for them where the dangers appeared, threatening their holiness and service for Christ. And all this took courage on his part because it was not an easy message to give. It was a message of warning, which is not always well received by those whom we lead.

One has to remember Paul's words to the Ephesian elders in Acts 20. It was not just a first line of leadership and teaching, but rather the kind of leadership and teaching which could be reproduced in the lives of subordinates. Who would warn the church about the apostates after Jude was gone? Obviously, those to whom he was writing and with whom he had spent time in order to reproduce his own leadership in their lives.

Apostasy and the True Believers

> But ye, beloved, building up yourselves on your most holy faith, praying in the Holy Ghost, keep yourselves in the love of God, looking for the mercy of our Lord Jesus Christ unto eternal life. And of some have compassion, making a difference: and others save with fear, pulling them out of the fire; hating even the garment spotted by the flesh. Now unto him that is able to keep you from falling, and to present you faultless before the presence of his glory with exceeding joy. To the only wise God our Saviour, be glory and majesty, dominion and power, both now and ever (Jude 20-25).

The responsibility of the saints to take leadership in a difficult situation emerges immediately. A wise leader builds himself up against the error of false teaching by learning and living in the truth. He prays by means of the Holy Spirit. He keeps himself in the love of God. He looks for the future immortality and glorification of eternal life.

Meanwhile, he reaches out to those who are caught in the tide of sin and confusion and reaches them. First he preaches love; but if that fails, he preaches judgment, clearly snatching them out of the fire.

Jude 22-23 has been variously interpreted by commentators down through the years. The New International Version translates these verses: "Be merciful to those who doubt; snatch others from the fire and save them; to others show mercy, mixed with fear–hating even the clothing stained by corrupted flesh."

So the leader fighting apostasy is actually grappling with three groups of people: those who doubt, those who seem to show no interest at all in spiritual things and must be snatched from the fire, and those who need a mixture of mercy and fear.

There is an interesting outline which emerges from Jude 1:20-25, helping us to communicate this portion of the Book of Jude to others. Perhaps it will be useful to you in the preparation of a sermon, a Sunday school lesson, or a home Bible study.

I. Personal Edification (vv. 20-21)
II. Personal Evangelism (vv. 22-23)
III. Personal Encouragement (vv. 24-25)

The theme for leadership is very clear. One's task begins with building himself up spiritually (personal edification). Then he is responsible for reaching out to others, only after he has dealt with apostasy in the church (personal evangelism). But all this is dependent on the continual ministry of the Lord in the life of the Christian leader (personal encouragement).

Jude certainly did not presume that the believer could accomplish all this alone, but showed how God keeps us from falling, presents us someday faultless before Himself, and deserves praise for what He is and what He does.

Jude 24 is one of the great promises of the New Testament. God is able to keep His people from falling. He is able to present them eventually without any sin in the very presence of His own glory, at which time all will be joyful. So the sad ministry of warning and accusation will actually end in an atmosphere of joy when the apostates can no longer harm the people of God.

Ministry "against the odds" is worth it after all!

Footnotes

Chapter Two

[1]James M. Boice, *How God Can Use Nobodies* (Wheaton, Illinois: Victor Books, 1974) pp. 59-60.

[2]Dewey Beegle, *Moses the Servant of Yahweh* (Grand Rapids, Michigan: Eerdmans, 1972), p. 56.

[3]James G. Murphy, *Commentary on Exodus* (New York: I. K. Funk and Company, 1881), p. 30.

[4]William S. LaSor, *Great Personalities of the Old Testament* Westwood, New Jersey: Fleming H. Revell, 1959), p. 64.

Chapter Three

[1]*Ibid.*, p. 57.

[2]J. Donald Phillips, "What Do You Think About Your Delegation Practices?" *The Hillsdale Report,* 12, No. 2, p. 5.

[3]J. P. Hyatt, *New Century Bible* (Greenwood, South Carolina: Attic Press, 1971), p. 194.

Chapter Four

[1]Alan Redpath, *Victorious Christian Living* (Westwood, New Jersey: Fleming H. Revell, 1955), p. 30.

[2]*Ibid.*, pp. 33-34.

[3]LaSor, *op. cit.*, p. 69.

Chapter Five

[1]Rudolf Kittel, *Great Men and Movements in Israel* (Library of Biblical Studies, KTAV, 1968), p. 65.

[2]James Hastings, *The Greater Men and Women of the Bible* (London: T and T Clark, 1913), pp. 467-468.

Chapter Six

[1]Edith Deen, *All of the Women of the Bible* (New York: Harper and Row, 1955), p. 70.

[2]Hastings, *op. cit.*, p. 446.

[3]Hastings, *op. cit.*, p. 455.

[4]Kittel, *op. cit.*, p. 60.

Chapter Eight

[1]LaSor, *op. cit.*, p. 109.

[2]Boice, *op. cit.*, p. 112.

Chapter Nine

[1]Alfred Edersheim, *Bible History*, Vol. V (Grand Rapids, Michigan: Eerdmans, 1954), p. 64.

[2]Samuel Matthews, Winfield Parks, and Robert C. Magis, "The Phoenicians: Sea Lords of Antiquity," *National Geographic*, Aug. 1974, p. 123.

Chapter Ten

[1]Merrill F. Unger, *Introductory Guide to the Old Testament* (Grand Rapids, Michigan: Zondervan, 1951).

[2]Kenneth O. Gangel, *Leadership for Church Education* (Chicago: Moody Press, 1970), p. 267.

Chapter Eleven

[1]Robert D. Culver, unpublished teaching notes on the Book of Daniel, Trinity Evangelical Divinity School, Deerfield, Illinois.

Chapter Twelve

[1]D. Edmond Hiebert, "Scribes, Jewish," *Zondervan Pictorial Encyclopedia of the Bible*, ed. Merrill C. Tenney (Grand Rapids, Michigan: Zondervan, 1963), p. 761.

[2]LaSor, *op. cit.*, pp. 181-182.

[3]Unger, *op. cit.*, p. 126.

Chapter Fourteen

[1]Stephen Neill, *What We Know About Jesus* (Grand Rapids, Michigan: Eerdmans, 1972), p. 23.

[2]William S. LaSor, *Great Personalities of the New Testament* (Westwood, New Jersey: Fleming H. Revell, 1961), p. 46.

Chapter Fifteen

[1]*Ibid.*, p. 81.

Chapter Sixteen

[1]Charles John Ellicott, *A New Testament Commentary,* Vol. II (London: Cassell and Company, 1897), p. 37.

Chapter Seventeen

[1]Henry Jacobsen, *The Acts Then and Now* (Wheaton, Illinois: Victor Books, 1973), p. 121.

Chapter Eighteen

[1]Richard Longenecker, *The Ministry and Message of Paul* (Grand Rapids, Michigan: Zondervan, 1971), p. 24.

[2]Jacobsen, *op. cit.,* p. 165.

Chapter Nineteen

[1]Emil G. Kraeling, *The Rand McNally Bible Atlas* (Chicago: Rand McNally and Company, 1956), p. 441.

[2]Kenneth O. Gangel, "Paul's Areopagus Speech," *Bibliotheca Sacra,* Oct. 1970, p. 312.

[3]Longenecker, *op. cit.,* p. 111.

[4]John Pollack, *The Man Who Shook the World* (Wheaton, Illinois: Victor Books, 1972), p. 116.

Chapter Twenty-One

[1]J. B. Lightfoot, *The Epistles of St. Paul* (New York: Macmillan and Company, 1879), p. 2.

[2]*Ibid.,* p. 29.

[3]A. T. Robertson, *Paul and the Intellectuals* (Nashville: Broadman, 1956), p. 138.

Chapter Twenty-Two

[1]E. M. Blaiklock, "Philemon," *Zondervan Pictorial Bible Dictionary,* ed. Merrill C. Tenney (Grand Rapids, Michigan: Zondervan, 1963), p. 649.

[2]J. B. Lightfoot, *Epistle to Philemon* (New York: Macmillan and Company, 1879), pp. 311-312.

Chapter Twenty-Three

[1]David O. Moberg, "The Nature and Needs of Older Adults," *Adult Education in the Church,* eds. Roy B. Zuck and Gene A. Getz (Chicago: Moody Press, 1970), p. 57.

[2]E. M. Blaiklock, *Letters to Children of Light* (Glendale, California: Regal, 1975), p. 7.

[3]LaSor, *op. cit.,* pp. 165-166.

[4]Kenneth O. Gangel, *You and Your Spiritual Gifts* (Chicago: Moody Press, 1974), p. 83.

[5]John R. W. Stott, *The Epistles of John* (Grand Rapids, Michigan: Eerdmans, 1964), p. 41.

Chapter Twenty-Four

[1]Kenneth O. Gangel, *The Gospel and the Gay* (Nashville: Thomas Nelson Publishing Company, 1978).